INTUITION ON DEMAND

A step-by-step guide
to powerful intuition
you can trust

Lisa K. PhD

 FINDHORN PRESS

INTUITION
ON DEMAND

A step-by-step guide
to powerful intuition
you can trust

Lisa K. PhD

 FINDHORN PRESS

Findhorn Press
One Park Street
Rochester, Vermont 05767
www.findhornpress.com

Findhorn Press is a division of Inner Traditions International

ISBN 978-1-84409-719-7

Cataloging-in-Publication Data for this title is available from the British Library

Printed and bound in the United States

Edited by Michael Hawkins
Cover design by Richard Crookes
Text design and layout by Damian Keenan

Contents

. . . .

What Intuition Can Do for You

• • • • • • • • • • • • •

When I was 27 years old, I vividly remember sitting in the back seat of a car looking out the window as we drove out of the hospital parking lot when all of a sudden I had butterflies in my stomach. My brother was driving and my mom sat in front. We had just left my 68-year-old dad's bedside right after he had come out of quintuple bypass heart surgery. The doctors had said he was fine and the operation was a success. Even in the waiting room during the surgery I was a bit tense, but not nervous and my stomach was calm. Exiting the parking lot, as the butterflies rose in my stomach I thought this very odd, and even said aloud, "I'm more nervous now than I was when Dad was in the operating room!" I hadn't had butterflies in my stomach since I was 10 years old playing the violin for an audience of parents at a school concert. This was very strange.

When we arrived at my parent's house a message on the answering machine from the hospital said to call them back right away. Mom called immediately. The doctor told her that just after we had left, my Dad's blood pressure dropped to dangerous levels. They thought he was bleeding inside so they took him back into surgery to check. They discovered he wasn't bleeding but was having an allergic reaction to the medication they gave him. His blood pressure had been so low for so long, coupled with the additional anesthesia to put him under again, that the doctors worried he might not wake up again from brain damage. They said the only thing we could do now was wait and see if he woke up.

After we heard the news, my brother and I decided to stay overnight with Mom. It took me a while to fall asleep. The butterflies were still fluttering around in my stomach and I was now truly tense with worry. Eventually, I did fall asleep and I dreamt about my Dad sitting at the dinner table all well and animated. In the dream he was telling us how his bypass surgery was a breeze as if nothing unusual happened to which I replied, "No, it wasn't a breeze, you don't understand!" And then I woke up. Lying in bed for a while I still felt the butterflies in my stomach. About ten minutes later, the butterflies disappeared! I went into my Mom's room and said, "I think Dad is going to be okay," when the phone rang. It was the hospital nurse, she said Dad was starting to wake up, and was wiggling his toes.

Dad was okay and he fully recovered with no brain damage. I was relieved though I felt stunned, not just from the upsetting incident, but it made me wonder, was I getting signals and messages about his condition before anyone told me about it? How could this happen? Was it intuition?

The World We Live in Is Insecure and Uncertain

Things happen in our lives that are not pleasant and sometimes downright scary. You want to navigate through life with some control and assurance that things will be okay or that the choices you make will alleviate further pain or not make things worse. Making those decisions is hard when the future is uncertain and unknown. Then there are the times when there is nothing to decide but only sit and wait. Sitting and waiting can be torture. Intuition can give us a glimmer of hope, solace and guidance during difficult times.

The problem is intuition seems to be random and elusive. More commonly, intuition seems vague and intangible. You may often wonder whether you even have intuition, much less have it under your control. Many people who want to develop their intuition to be dependable often have the same motivation. They have had experiences where their undeveloped intuition has given them a rare stunning message or they feel their intuition is trying to tell them something, but they don't know what it is.

Whether you are going through wanting to improve day to day life or dealing with a life upheaval, you may often wish you had dependable internal guidance, a message or some grace from God letting you know things will be okay, that you are not alone or just assurances of the right thing to do next. You want that inner guidance, a connection to a knowing, that seems to know everything. What you want is consistent, reliable intuition on demand.

Developing Your Intuition Can Change Your World

If you want your intuition to be useful, you need to have control over it. Not to have your intuition tell you what you want to hear, but rather to use your intuition on what you want to know about. Whether you want to make better decisions in choosing the right action to take, picking the best person, or deciding which direction to go in, you are always looking for guidance in your decisions. You seek the best knowing to allay your fears. To do this, you need to use your intuition on what you want, when you want, and get enough detailed information so you can use what you received. With a strong intuition you can build confidence in your life that you are always supported, have strong guidance that you can rely upon and feel safe.

The techniques and methods in this book answer the most common questions that I've found many people and you may have about intuition. Those common questions are:

- How do I make my intuition happen when I want and use it for what I want rather than it happening randomly?
- How do I know it's my intuition giving me a message and that I'm not just making it up?
- What I'm getting from my intuition is vague and I'm not sure what it means; how do I get more detailed and meaningful information from my intuition?

Intuition On Demand answers all of these questions for you and more as it takes you stepwise through a down to earth, tangible process that makes sense. You'll find the approach to intuition here is not "woo woo" but is straightforward and understandable. These techniques were built upon research and personal experience using them with hundreds of people with great success. In addition, you can apply the techniques to any situation and build upon them for what you personally need.

The ultimate goal of developing your intuition with these techniques and methods is to be intuitive all the time so you know your warning and guidance system is always running. Leading an intuitive life can bring you great joy and happiness when you can use your intuition on demand.

Lisa K.
Briarcliff Manor, NY
January 2017

PART ONE

Demystifying Intuition

CHAPTER 1

Intuition On Demand –
Making Intuition Tangible
and Why This Works

• • • • • • • • • • • • •

From a young age you are told how to think by your parents, guiding you to do the right thing, and as you grow older you are surrounded and bombarded by others telling you again how to think, constantly persuading you on what to be, do or which direction to go in. You become accustomed to looking for others to give you solutions that are right for you, when you already have the best intuitive problem solver in the world, right inside your head. You just need to undo your trained way of thinking and use all information that is available to you. Gathering information from both – from outside sources and inside of you – where you can use both your logic and your intuition, is a better way to move in your life.

There are fantastic intuitive solutions that are carved out especially for you that nothing can compare with, residing inside a part of your mind that most people don't access. That part of your mind is a function of your brain that has connections to vast unseen knowledge. When you access those solutions and that knowledge, magical and amazing things can happen just for you, to do with what you wish.

How awesome is that?

Discovery of the Intuition On Demand Technique

I never considered myself to be intuitive. I didn't have experiences that others who teach about psychic and intuition development had as young children. I wasn't seeing spirits, nor was I getting amazing intuitive messages as a child. Other than the butterflies in my stomach experience with my Dad's surgery in my 20s, and one other intuitive message that helped me with a friend's crisis, I ceased having intuitive messages. It wasn't that I didn't try to use my intuition. It just didn't work for me when I wanted it to.

Often my intuition seemed like it didn't work at all. Decades later I learned how to develop my intuition through extensive research, study and training so my intuition was under my control to use "on demand." Unintentionally I found myself doing intuitive readings for the public and to my surprise, my appointment slots sold out at events. My skills improved and later, my intuition actually saved my life when I needed it.

It was the middle of the night and I woke up shaking uncontrollably. I knew something was very wrong and asked my husband to call the ambulance. The emergency room doctors performed some tests and discovered I had bacteria in my blood, but they told me, "You're not shaking anymore, so you can go home now. See your doctor in the morning."

The next morning my doctor did what doctors normally do, he gave me antibiotic pills. The medication didn't work and every day I would have bouts of my heart racing and shortness of breath while I was lying down in bed. I didn't know what was happening and my intuitive feeling was this wasn't good.

Another attack happened again, which was so bad I thought I was going to pass out and my hands turned white. I called 911, and went back to the emergency room. I told the doctor, "It's getting worse, I'm short of breath and my heart is pounding, my hands turned white, what is that?" The doctor replied, "Oh, you were hyperventilating, that was fear." I told him, "I really don't think so. I wasn't afraid, this is something more than that." But the doctor insisted and said, "No, just go home, continue to take your medicine and you'll be fine."

Almost in desperation I turned to my intuition to find out more from my inner guidance and I was "told" that I was seriously ill but if I found an infectious disease specialist, I would be okay. It was the weekend and my calls to find a new infectious disease doctor were unanswered and I was continuing to feel worse. My intuition then guided me to read a book on my shelf about how to find the best pediatrician. It was a bit odd, but I started to read it anyway. As I read the book, the word pediatrician kept coming up over and over again. I thought, "Wait a minute, I have a pediatrician friend and he's my neighbor. Maybe he knows of someone who could help me!"

I picked up the phone to dial, then in my head my intuition pops this message, "He's away on vacation but he'll be back later, leave a detailed message." So I dialed the phone and when he didn't pick up, I left a detailed message. Later that afternoon he called me back and said, "I was away on vacation, I just came home and got your message. I know exactly what you need to do, you need to see an infectious disease specialist and I know one who will see you right away. I am going to message him now and he will see you."

I saw the specialist the next day and after he received the blood test results he said, "Yes, not only do you still have bacteria in your blood but you also have a heart infection." He then put me in the hospital.

After six weeks of intravenous antibiotics I was cured. I realized, had I not gotten the intuitive message to get help right away and to not listen to those other doctors that were saying "You're okay, just go home," I don't know whether I'd be here today. A heart infection, or endocarditis, can often be rapidly fatal without treatment. I am also relieved that I didn't have any heart damage from it. I thank my intuitive guidance for saving my life. This is the main reason I teach others to develop their intuition, because it can help them in important ways in their life, as it has for me.

Through my studies and experience in performing over 500 intuitive readings I had finally figured out a system and technique that made my intuition work consistently and reliably. It worked exceedingly well, as I later discovered, not only for myself but also for others. These techniques and system make up the core of this book.

People's Success with the Intuition On Demand Technique

I began to share and teach this knowledge first in monthly intuition development meetings, initially with friends and then with others who were interested. Over time, the group grew to over a total of 150 students who had some amazing results. They were from all walks of life: doctors, lawyers, professionals and stay at home moms. Some would share their stories with me. Here is one from George, an average hard working fellow who works in television.

> "Friday night, I had the [intuitive] sense of a freezing pipe, I then checked on the boiler, to find it had stopped working! The fuel line was frozen! If I had not checked... Would have gone to bed... Lots of frozen pipes would have been the outcome! You and your teachings have been a gift!"

Soon, what I taught evolved into a two-day workshop called Developing Your Intuition, Level One and then another called Advanced Intuition Development. I expanded the workshop's reach by offering it as an online class to students around the globe from Asia to Europe, Canada and all over the United States. At the same time, I began to lecture and publicly speak on some of the intuition methods and techniques. The response to the talks was very well received, and some people in the audience immediately had results from what they learned, even on the way home. Using the information that Allison learned from attending one of my talks, she wrote to me:

> "Thank you so much for your lecture at the New Life Expo. Having experienced all three days of the expo now, I can say that your lecture was one of my favorites. I have been practicing using my intuition, and I am so impressed how well it worked on the following: I knew which subway train would leave first. My intuition told me that a man on the subway would leave on a stop before me. I knew which seat a panelist would sit in (2nd from the left). [My intuition] said I would arrive at 8:41 pm, and sure enough, the train pulled into my home station at that exact time."

People enjoyed the way I explain techniques in a down to earth, step-by-step fashion that was tangible and easy for them to understand. They felt they could relate well to my being a more "grounded" person who was not "woo woo," particularly because of my background in science and engineering. In my speaking engagements, people would ask me what book they could read so they could learn more, and alas, I didn't have a book I could recommend that explained exactly what I taught. This is how this book started.

The Intuition Technique Based on Research, Studies and Experience

When I started to learn about developing my intuition, I initially searched out books on intuition that seemed logically and scientifically based. There were very few on how to develop intuition. Most of the written material that did discuss intuition was focused on proving that people believed in intuition and used theirs frequently. The only sources for intuition development were in the metaphysical genre. My approach was to be open and investigate a wide range of sources. I felt that if you are going to learn something you didn't know anything about and give it your all, you have to be open.

Using my background and education in the science of psychobiology I researched scientific studies on intuition, extra sensory perception and psychic phenomenon. Reading scientific journals with studies and research on intuition to books on intuition in business, I gathered a good broad view of intuition's proof of existence. I then moved to the metaphysical explorations, which centered on the world beyond the physical. This revealed an interesting correlation at certain points between the biology of the brain and cognition with the theories of metaphysical energy.

I even went on to study the ancient Chinese Traditional Medicine of Qigong, which is the basis for all energy healing modalities practiced today. I really wanted to understand it all, and get the broad picture of the intuition phenomenon so I then pursued degrees in Metaphysical Sciences. My PhD dissertation was written on human intuition.

Learning about intuition in theory only takes you so far, however. To actually understand it well you have to experience it. This makes it true for you and strengthens your understanding.

I've taken the best of all of my research, studies, a myriad of workshops and experience to help you develop your intuition with the most efficient and effective techniques that I found work for myself and other people. If you work your way through the material in this book and then diligently practice using your intuition, you will improve.

Why This Works and How It Is
Different From Other Books

When I first tried to learn how to work with my intuition, many of the books I read and classes I took were often confusing. The teacher or author would tell the reader or student that intuition "works with the unknown," or you need to be "conscious of your subconscious" — all of which left me baffled. Many courses and books on intuition and psychic development mainly focus on the "Clairs", chakras and human energy system. This was somewhat helpful, but still didn't explain how to make intuition appear when I needed it.

Dozens of articles written on how to improve your intuition will list meditation, connecting with nature and your feelings as the major steps. The rest, as they say, is left up to the reader to figure out. Unlike these books, *Intuition On Demand* explains a structured technique on how to go step-by-step to make intuition happen when you want, on what you want.

When you begin to learn how to work with your intuition you will go through the first step of getting bits and pieces of intuitive information that usually don't make sense. *Intuition On Demand* takes you to the next level by showing you how to get more detailed information from your intuition that is useful and can be understood and acted upon.

Intuition On Demand focuses on the process of getting intuitive information so it can work for you right away. Rather than debating or disputing where the intuitive information may be coming from we'll be focusing on getting your intuition to work for you at your command. Ultimately, it doesn't matter exactly where intuition comes from, whether it is from angels, your higher self, your subconscious, or the deep recesses of your brain that hold learned knowledge and experience, as long as it is working consistently and reliably with verifiable positive results.

This book also explains the importance of practicing, as well as giving you a good understanding of what makes a good intuition exercise from a bad one and the best way to do an intuition exercise. As seen from the success of many students already using the *Intuition On Demand* techniques and methods, you can be confident you can get similar results on your own.

Who This Book Is For

If you are the kind of person who likes to have the complex broken down into simple easy to understand concepts, then this book is for you. Intuition is presented here from the "every day" person's point of view. The approach here is to be less "woo woo", more logically and, where possible, science based. We will cover metaphysics from the energy standpoint and show how to manage metaphysical energy and your own human energy field because energy is a central component to the metaphysical science behind intuition.

Studies have shown that intuition is used by many of us whether we are aware of it or not. Intuition is often difficult for people to describe in themselves, and often intuition's influence on their behavior is subconscious. At other times people know that their intuition is telling them to act and though they can't explain why, are compelled to follow its message. In business, intuition plays an important role in management plans and actions.

Surveying my own students and those I coach privately, I find they often have similar problems with their intuition. The techniques in this book can solve their problems.

Here are some of their comments:

"I want to really trust my intuition and get clear messages."

"I want to know my guides and angels better. I want to feel that someone's got my back and they are there with me, that I can talk to them."

"I would like to use my intuition to help me make good decisions and be able to connect to that part of me."

"I've had some successes with my intuition, but it feels like it is just below the surface, and I can't quite get over this hump to move forward. I feel kind of stuck."

"Sometimes I don't receive clear messages. Sometimes, it's really clear, sometimes, it's not. I think it's from a lack of trust on my part, because I don't always trust my intuition. I'm always second-guessing myself. So for me, that is my biggest frustration."

"I want to get back to center, because when I'm out of center I know it impedes my intuition."

They are seeking to improve their intuition so they can:

- Reduce anxiety
- Gain confidence
- Always feel supported
- Always feel connected
- Feel safer
- Reduce fear in their lives
- Make the best decisions
- Be divinely guided and connected all the time

Definitions of Terms

Working with intuition is often a new adventure for people. To help with some terms that may be unfamiliar here are some definitions.

A HIT   *When you correctly have received the intuitive message and it can be verified it was right.*

A MISS   *An intuitive message is misinterpreted or you have not picked up the intuitive message correctly.*

INTUITIVE READER   *person who gives intuitive information they are receiving about someone else, to them, for guidance.*

SITTER   *A person who is getting an intuitive reading from someone else.*

READER   *The person who is doing the intuitive reading for someone else.*

How to Use This Book

From my own experience in learning to develop my intuition from scratch as well as teaching hundreds of students, I've discovered the pitfalls and problems you may encounter that may prevent you from making quick progress. Below are the most common problems that people experience as they practice using their intuition and how to address them.

1. Not practicing. – You need to practice! I can't emphasize this enough! Don't just read the book and then immediately try to use your intuition on life problems right away. This is like reading the driver's manual to learn how to drive, and then getting out on the highway without practice driving. Practice makes perfect, or at least a whole lot better!

2. Being afraid of being wrong. – Be brave! Just spit it out. Throw it out there. Whatever you get is fine. In the beginning you have to expect that you will have misses. It's okay to miss. Often the most astounding hits people receive are things they thought were ridiculous or that they were making up. You have to push through your fear of being wrong to practice intuition.

3. Trying to make everything you get fit to be a hit. – Intuitive hits are often obvious; if you are stretching too much to make it fit, then it's not a hit. Misses are okay (see #2).

4. Giving up because nothing you get fits as a hit. – Often I have found that students have an expectation of what their hits are supposed to be like, or mean. You may actually be getting hits but don't see the connection. Don't give up your practicing! Stick to it and you will see results.

5. Missed expectations – Expecting immense detail and stunning results right away will disappoint you.

6. Comparing yourself to others. – The worst thing you can do is compare your results to other people's. We all progress at different rates, and we all have times when we have a string of hits, or sometimes amazing hits, and then we don't. It's all okay, whatever you receive is fine.

7. Saying, "I know that already" and skimming through the material. – The biggest learning killer is to assume that you have learned it all already. Having a different perspective of material you may have been exposed to is always beneficial as concepts you thought you understood suddenly become clearer.

The technique is key to improving your intuition as you will be using it over and over again in different scenarios. As you practice you'll be working with it to build your skill. Any good technique needs to be stepwise and repeatable. You will also need to repeat it. As you use a technique you can apply the technique in different ways. Later I will show you those different applications which I call tools, that will help expand your skill to advance to intermediate and advanced levels. The technique will become second nature to you.

If you don't believe or like the metaphysics here you can skip it. The metaphysics helps expand your understanding and is included here for those who are interested. If you don't believe, just skip the chapters. However, if like me you want a rounded, broad immersion on intuition then read with an open mind.

The book is in 5 parts. Part 1 is on demystifying intuition so you can work with it. Part 2 breaks down the Intuition On Demand technique in detail and includes the Intuition Toolkit and how to apply them step-by-step. Part 3 focuses on intuition exercises that you can do alone or with a partner, and how to practice properly. Part 4 explains the metaphysics of intuition energy and includes two most important mindsets and practices that you can do to accelerate your intuition growth. Finally, Part 5 shows you how to live an intuitive life and answers frequently asked questions.

Intuition is the key that unlocks all doors beyond which are the places you want to go, the things you want to have and ultimately lead you to the life you want to lead. Are you ready to step into a new world? Let's go and see how intuition can give you an advantage in life.

CHAPTER 2

What is Intuition?

. . . .

Intuition Definition

Teaching you about developing your intuition will work best if we briefly define what intuition is first, so you have a clear understanding of what I'm referring to and also what you're working with.

A simple definition of intuition is, "knowing without knowing how you know it." Most often the source of intuitive knowledge is seen as coming from one of two places. One perspective is the source of intuition is a subconscious process that produces internal information you've experienced, gathered, processed at some point and perhaps forgotten, that is not conscious. The other perspective is it is information that comes from mystical sources, outside of you, such as from your higher self, angels, spirit guides or divine consciousness.

For the purposes of this book, while it doesn't really matter where the information is coming from, as long as it is accurate and useful, intuition will be viewed here as giving you information from both inside and outside of you. In general, you don't really know where intuitive information comes from. But, if you can harness its power and increase its effectiveness to help make better decisions and create a better life that you desire then let's do that! My personal belief is that we are tapping into a source of knowledge and information that is beyond us. As you'll see later in the book, this belief actually helps improve the accuracy of your intuition and I'll explain why.

I've always been fascinated with how the mind works and that motivated me to study psychology. I quickly discovered there is a lot more we don't know about how the mind works than what we do know. My psychology textbooks did not even mention intuition and certainly never how it works. One thing psychology does acknowledge is intuition does exist and everyone is intuitive; there are no exceptions. Everyone can develop his or her intuition skill to become highly intuitive.

10 Key Secrets to Intuition

When I first started learning about intuition I had no idea what intuition felt like, how intuition came to people. Intuition always seemed magical, that it was an instant download of encyclopedic information or deep insightful understanding. It looked as if people became instant geniuses with intuitively manifested information. Highly intuitive people seemed to have a knowing that was like telling a story, it was incredible. Since I believe that psychics are people with an advanced intuition skill, it seemed what they received psychically and intuitively appeared to them as if they were repeating detailed information that was being dictated to them.

What I discovered is that intuition doesn't come to anyone like that at all. After researching intuition and studying highly skilled psychics, both observing them closely and receiving readings from some world famous intuitive readers, I realized what was actually happening. In fact, when they apply a technique to receive and work with intuitive messages, they can produce highly detailed information that seems like someone was dictating a story to them. The first step is to understand some key secrets to intuition.

Intuition is not reasoning, deduction or rationalizing a conclusion nor "coming up" with a solution. So, what is intuition like? How does intuition come to you? How do you facilitate accessing your intuition? How do you know intuition when you experience it? The first step to answering those questions is knowing some important characteristics of intuition so you can begin to recognize it. I call these the 10 Key Secrets to Intuition.

1. Be Relaxed and Be Open

This first secret is really important in being able to receive intuitive information easily, and with clarity; it's for you to be receptive and passive. Be open to what you will receive because the information isn't coming from your thinking mind, it's not something that you may even expect. Being open to receive is the golden key here. Intuitive answers are guidance, so be open to whatever you get. Whatever you receive is okay. When you are uptight, or worried about what you are going to receive, intuitive messages are going to be harder to recognize. This is why it is important to be calm and not emotional. Be relaxed and open.

You can think to yourself that you'll now be receiving guidance, "I will be open to receive, whatever guidance that comes." Intuitive messages often guide you to an answer; they do not always to tell you what to do. Don't be anxious or tense about getting an intuitive message. One will come; it always does because you are always thinking, feeling, seeing, hearing and aware. I have a picture in my mind that symbolizes this: visualize that you are sitting in a big easy chair relaxed and being open to whatever appears before you.

If you are anxious, fearful, angry or otherwise highly emotional you won't be able to distinguish your intuition speaking to you from your emotional thoughts. The same thing goes for being too excited or exuberant. You may be too eager to get the result that you want, so you look for a particular positive result. Your intuitive messages will be neutral and non-emotional. You need to be non-emotional to receive them clearly.

2. No Figuring It Out, No Judging the Answer

The second secret is "No figuring it out, no judging the answer." The biggest inhibitor of intuition is our thinking and judging mind. Our Ego is the culprit behind our judgment and it will get our analyzing mind engaged in the process. This is one of the harder aspects to work with because you'll always want to examine and over- think about what you're receiving. Sometimes you may be impatient to get a message that solves your problem immediately, or you're looking for the epiphany, the, "Aha! I've got it!" This causes you to try to guess what the message means. You must resist doing this. It is important to remember that our Ego and thinking mind is 100% *NON* intuitive.

When you first start developing your intuition the first intuitive message you receive often doesn't make sense. This is because of the way intuition "speaks" to us in pieces. You have to gather several pieces to see what the message truly means. When you receive your first intuitive message, because you don't understand it, you judge it. When we judge, we corrupt the message. Remember, the messages are coming from outside of us or from sources that we are not aware of, so we don't know exactly what it's going to say. Also, trying to judge it and figure it out may lead us to the wrong conclusion, or worse, in the wrong direction. Your intuitive messages will come in pieces and as they do they will reveal the message they are conveying. I'll explain how to gather the pieces later in the intuition techniques.

3. Fragments and Symbols

Intuitive messages do not involve thinking. Often if it appears through thought, it is a concept that pops up or just a few words. The intuitive message is not a "thought out" long explanation. Intuitive messages will come to you in bits and pieces. Intuitive messages are short, fleeting, and piecemeal; they often feel or seem like fragments. Later I will explain how you can get more information from these fragments and pieces. So just take the intuitive answer as it is. Remember, you will not always get full detailed information, later the pieces will fit together to make sense. Also, more often you will be given pointers to the next step, and not always the big picture or solution.

Intuitive information comes in symbols and representations of meaning. This is because the intuitive part of your mind speaks in symbols, not in words. These symbols are uniquely yours. This is because your mind doesn't just think in words and sentences but also in symbols that are representations of concepts, expressions, feelings, states of mind or being, situations, etc. You may not be aware of what your symbols are because you don't often use them when you communicate with someone. You can build your personal lexicon or dictionary of symbols through using your intuition frequently. You'll begin to associate your intuitive symbols with their meaning as you practice your intuition exercises.

4. Signs Outside of You

Just as your intuition can draw your attention to notice things in your environment as part of its message to you, your intuition can also point out signs outside of you as well. You may be thinking, "How can my intuition make a sign appear outside of me?" Since the Universe is connected to you and everything in it is part of one energy mass, the Universe can bring you signs that can be a message for you. Synchronicity can make the right things, people and situations appear at the right time not only to be a guidepost to point you in the right direction, but they can also be part of an intuitive message. These signs can be very clear messages outside of you; road signs, license plates, literal signs on a wall, a headline on a newspaper or magazine, a book title or real people who serve as Earth Angels can give you a message too.

An Earth Angel can be anyone you happen to encounter who just happens to tell you what you need to hear at that moment. Someone who probably doesn't even know they are being an Earth Angel or that they are an indirect messenger. You may overhear a conversation that has relevance to you or your situation. Perhaps it gives you the answer you're looking for. An Earth Angel may be a friend who tells you just what you needed to hear at the right moment. It is important to recognize that sometimes the sign is just a pointer to send you to the right place to get more information. You have to follow it to find out what the complete message is. You may be guided to read a book, an article, to go talk to a particular person, visit a place, or go to an event or do an activity.

5. Believing = Power

When you believe that intuition exists and that everyone, including you, can access it, your intuitive power increases. The energy booster of intuition is belief and trust. Your doubt about your intuitive ability saps the energy behind being successful at it. While you may find doubting yourself to be the most difficult, just know it takes practice and experience to get over your doubt. The more you experience your intuition by working through, improving your skill by practicing, the stronger your trust will be.

All highly intuitive people have gone through periods of doubt, especially when they are starting to build their intuition skills. But, learning how to strengthen your intuition is like any other skill, such as tennis or golf. It takes a lot of practice to be confident and trust that you can serve the ball accurately in the serve box, or hit a long drive down the middle of the fairway. If you drive a car, do you remember when you first learned how to drive? You didn't always trust your ability to drive through traffic without hitting another car. Because you have had years of practice and experience driving, you no longer doubt your ability to avoid hitting other cars. You just drive. The same goes for intuition skill building. Just trust that your intuition works, that you can receive an intuitive answer. You have to *believe* that you will and are receiving intuitive messages! That allows you to let go and let it happen.

6. Outside Tools

Sometimes we can use a little help. Outside tools, as opposed to the methods you use inside your mind, are traditionally called divination tools. Some examples of tools would be angel or tarot card decks, numerology, palmistry, runes, I-Ching or even tea leaves. There is no magic in these tools. They are just tools to help you get out of your Ego mind and into a state of mind where you are more open to what your intuition is telling you. This also helps stimulate your mind to becoming more aware of the things going on in the intuitive part of your brain.

7. Trigger Your Intuition By Asking

One of the biggest myths about intuitive information is that it just appears to you randomly. I always wondered how people made their intuition actually happen on what they want. This is particularly key when someone comes to you for an intuitive reading! They will have lots of questions for you to get messages for them.

You can trigger your intuition by asking a question. Just as your thinking mind will always try to respond, your intuition will always respond. You can ask questions about anything. For example, you can ask where there is an open parking spot, what the best thing is to eat for lunch on the menu and so on. You can ask for help with anything, even before you know what it is you want. In this instance you can ask for a message for the best outcome and for your highest good.

8. You Get What You Get And You Don't Get Upset

This key secret is, "You get what you get and you don't get upset" which is also, "Let go to receive." When you are looking for divine guidance from your intuition, you may struggle with wanting a particular outcome or have an urge to try to "figure out" a more complex meaning or story behind what you receive. It is important that you resist doing this. Whatever you receive does not need to be modified, interpreted nor changed. This is because your intuition is giving you a message in pieces. You will receive one piece at a time, each in response to a question you ask it. Those pieces will form the message for you.

The harder you push to get an intuitive message, the more elusive it becomes. When you try too hard, your thinking mind comes into play. You will start to judge and try to come up with a meaning to the message. Remember, that the intuitive message is not coming from your thinking mind. Whatever you get as an answer to your question is fine. Going beyond just "being open," this attitude of "you get what you get and don't get upset" helps set your mindset and prepares you for whatever your intuition gives you.

31

Your intuitive message may take some time to put together through gathering the intuitive pieces. Accepting what you receive helps your intuition convey a clear message without you corrupting it. Having an attitude of getting whatever you get and accepting it helps hone your intuition skill. Many of my students have told me this is one of the best "secrets" as it has helped them tremendously increase the accuracy in receiving their intuitive messages.

9. Ask For Clarity

When you first ask your intuition a question, especially when you are first learning, you probably won't understand what the answer means. If you don't understand the message you can ask again, and ask for clarity. This means asking your intuition another question based on the first message you received. For example, you may receive from your intuition the color blue, or an image of the sky pops in your mind. That doesn't make much sense in response to your question, so you ask another question about the color blue, "Why are you showing me the color blue, or the sky?" This will trigger your intuition to send you an answer to help clarify the message.

When you first see a psychic or intuitive reader work, it looks as if they're receiving an encyclopedia of intuitive knowledge in their messages. You may have asked them a question and they look at their cards (or not) then give you a long answer to your question. What they're not telling you is their process. They're asking their intuition, their guides or angels for more information about the symbols, the fragments and pieces of intuitive messages that they are receiving. Then when the full picture has formed for them, they relay that completed story to you.

I discovered this through watching many highly skilled psychics and intuitives' work. I studied, in depth, how to develop psychic skills and become an accurate reader. Watching the masters closely and seeing how they receive information I discovered that they aren't getting downloads of encyclopedic information; they are receiving clues, pieces and symbols. You have to work with these to get the big picture and the entire message. I'll explain how to do this later in the book.

10. "Where's the bathroom?"

The last key secret to intuition is the most important, the *pièce de résistance* in this entire list. It is "Where's the bathroom?" Okay, it's not actually where the bathroom is, but rather the state of mind you are in when you ask the question. When you are visiting a new place, say a restaurant or you're in someone's house for the first time, and you need to go to the bathroom, you ask the question, "Where's the bathroom?" You really need to go to the bathroom, so you are open for the answer, you're not second-guessing what they're going to tell you, and normally you don't judge what they tell you. You're open and waiting, listening for what they have to say. When you get the answer you go with it.

This is the state of mind you need to be in when you ask your intuition a question. You're open, you are quiet, listening carefully and paying attention and you don't judge what you get. Plus, you usually say, "Thank you" and go to the bathroom. When you have this same frame of mind after you ask your intuition a question, you are then open to whatever comes, and your mind is quiet. This allows you to receive your intuitive messages more clearly and without the clutter of your thinking mind getting in the way.

These ten key secrets to intuition are illuminating concepts and characteristics that introduce you to what intuition is, how it works and how you receive intuitive information. I will elaborate more on these again throughout the book, as it is important to keep them in mind as you learn the techniques to work with your intuition to strengthen and improve your skills.

The Difference Between Being Intuitive and Psychic

While waiting for the dentist, the dental assistant and I were just chit chatting about nothing in particular when she asked what do I do? I reluctantly told her that I did angel card readings. She wanted to know what an angel reading was, and so I explained that it was like a psychic reading but I connect to angels to give people messages. To my surprise, she became very enthusiastic about it and said she loves getting psychic readings. She envied people who were psychic and while she thought she was very intuitive, she said psychics were just amazingly gifted people. I explained to her, that I learned how to do this and that she could too. She said, "Oh no, my intuition is very good but, I could never do what you do, I'm not psychic. I could never do that, I'm not that special." Now when I travel to speak about intuition to any audience, large or small, I always ask them whether they think they are intuitive. Almost everyone raises his or her hand. I then ask, how many of you think you're psychic? And only a small few raise their hands.

Improving your ability to work with your intuition and developing your intuition skills are the basis for becoming a highly skilled psychic. On the spectrum of development, receiving some initial intuitive hits is just the beginning to becoming psychic. Again, intuition is the ability to understand something immediately, without conscious reasoning or knowing, i.e. "knowing without knowing how we know it." As you work with your intuition you can access more and more useful information that we cannot deduce logically or obtain just by thinking. This information can be extraordinary, it can tell you about the future, about people you haven't met, or places you haven't been to. In other words, intuition can give you information that would seem psychic.

But it's actually not mysterious, there is an explanation of how we are naturally intuitive and can become psychic looking at both science and metaphysics. I believe the best psychic and intuitive is someone who receives messages from a divine source, which could be considered the Universe and its creator, or whatever you believe in, that is full of goodness and love.

Most people believe they are intuitive or feel they have some intuition but don't believe they are psychic or could even be psychic. This belief often depends on what your definition of psychic is. For many people, being psychic seems to have a magical status that only special people have who were born with a gift that others were not blessed with. I have found that everyone no matter whether they believe they are slightly intuitive or not intuitive at all (like myself) can be psychic because I found that these techniques have helped many people go from being not intuitive or somewhat intuitive to being highly intuitive and even being clearly psychic.

So I definitely believe that you can do it too, and if you learn the techniques carefully, consistently practice, and exercise your intuition daily, you will develop your intuition until it will seem like you are psychic, because you will be.

What Intuition Is Not

Now that we've talked about what intuition is and its characteristics, let's talk about what intuition is not to clarify it even more. Intuition is not guessing, it is not deduction; it is not "figuring it out." Intuition is also not always knowledge that we have from accumulated experience. Intuition is not thinking but has very clear characteristics that parallel the way the right hemisphere of our brain works. You could say that this right side of our brain is the intuitive side.

Intuition Processing in Your Brain

The human mind is extremely complex, and so is the human brain. The study of the brain and how it functions gives us some clues about how our minds work. Both science and psychology still have much to figure out about intuition even though there has been a large amount of scientific research that has statistically proven the existence of human psychic abilities. However, the mind is still largely a mystery to us.

Later in the book, I will go more deeply into how the intuitive part of our brain works that can help you work with your intuition with clearer understanding and more accuracy.

Highlighted Tips and Summary

Intuition is defined as, "knowing without knowing how you know it." Intuition is *NOT* "figuring it out."

10 Key Secrets to Intuition:

1. Be Relaxed and Be Open
2. No Figuring It Out, No Judging the Answer
3. Fragments and Symbols
4. Signs Outside of You
5. Believing = Power
6. Outside Tools
7. Trigger Your Intuition By Asking
8. You Get What You Get and You Don't Get Upset
9. Ask for Clarity
10. "Where's the Bathroom?"

You can develop your intuition skill to become psychic. Your intuition is not deduction, experience or logic. "Where's the bathroom?" is key to being open to receiving your intuition clearly.

CHAPTER 3

The Intuition Learning Path: Where You Are on the 5-Step Map

• • • • • • • • • • • • •

When people first come to me wanting to learn about intuition, they usually already have had some intuitive experiences or received some intuitive messages but they can't tell if they made them up or not. Perhaps you've felt this way yourself. You can't articulate exactly what your intuitive feeling is and you often feel you are guessing about what your intuition is trying to tell you. The reason for this is because you are in the first step of the intuition learning process. The first step is recognizing you have some intuitive messages coming to you but they seem random and unclear. That's the good news; the next steps are to develop and grow your skill with your intuition, as you move along on the 5-Step Map of the Intuition Learning Path.

The 5-Step Map of the Intuition Learning Path is a process everyone goes through when developing his or her intuition. It is the step-by-step experience of how a novice becomes an incredible psychic medium or a young businessman learns to use his intuition to become a highly successful corporate giant. Knowing how the intuition learning process works helps accelerate and move your intuition skill to an advanced level quickly. When you know what step you are in you can take the proper action to move on to the next step after. I will explain each step in detail, with examples and give samples of people going through the process and what it's like.

5-Step Map of the Intuition Learning Path

STEP 1 *"In the Beginning" Intuition has caught your attention but seems random and uncontrollable.*

In the beginning you're like many other people who experience intuition the first few times. Perhaps you knew someone you love was in trouble before you were told. Maybe you were thinking about someone out of the blue and then they called or turned the corner in front of you as you walked down the street. You're surprised and wonder, "How did I know that?" Or perhaps you had a prophetic dream about a scary situation, and it later happened. Your intuition has now caught your attention because you've had some extraordinary intuitive experiences.

When my son, Chris, was about 6 years old, he ran to me one morning crying. I asked, "What's the matter?" He said, "Mommy, Mommy, I had a very, very bad dream. I dreamt that you were very sick and they took you away in an ambulance." He was so shaken, and as he never complained of bad dreams before, I was surprised. He hugged me so tightly. I reassured him, I wasn't sick and I didn't need to go anywhere in an ambulance.

Four years later, I had long forgotten his bad dream, when I came down with a sudden serious illness and had to be taken to the hospital in the middle of the night by ambulance. I ended up staying in the hospital for a long time with a heart infection. It was a very traumatic experience for Chris, being only 10 years old. What was more surprising was Chris reminded me of his very bad dream, and said that what happened in his dream actually happened in real life. From the policeman who first came to the house and stood in the hallway, to the paramedics who took me away, it was all exactly the same. He said his dream was the same right down to where he was sitting, what they said, how they were standing and what they looked like.

Most of us may not have such an extreme experience as this, but one like this would certainly make you a believer in intuition. It certainly made Chris a believer.

In this first step, you may find that your intuition seems to come and go. You believe that your intuitive messages are uncontrollable and seem to come to you at random. Perhaps you are completely unaware that you're actually receiving intuitive messages. You seem to know things that you can't place how you came to know it. This may be because your intuition is always working but you just don't know it or recognize it. The messages are often fleeting, subtle or only come in dreams. Sometimes looking back on it, you wonder if your intuitive experience was real or not. You may find out you're sensitive to energy, but you don't know it, and it manifests in your emotions or in your physical body as feeling ill or uneasy. Only later you discover that you have trouble being in large crowds or sitting next to certain people for no apparent reason.

STEP 2 *Beginner's Intuition. You try to pay attention to your intuition and figure out its messages but you don't understand them.*

In this second step, your intuitive experiences may have startled you or peaked your curiosity so much that you now have a strong desire to figure out if your intuition is sending you more messages. You wonder, what else could your intuition be telling you? Now you're interested in figuring it out and you try to pay attention. The problem is you get flashes of feelings or maybe even an image but you don't understand its meaning.

Now you try to pay attention to your intuition, you may try asking it a question and see how your intuition responds. But, instead of a satisfying answer, you get fragments in response to your question. You only get pieces of intuitive messages and they don't have much meaning. They seem disjointed and generate more questions.

One of the most common questions I'm asked is, "I know my intuition is telling me something. I keep ... seeing a face ... having a funny feeling... hearing a name ... How do I know what it means?" These people are in Step 2. What you're experiencing is a partially developed intuition plus you are getting other "noise" from your thinking mind or your Ego.

Your intuition is more noticeable to you because you are paying attention. That's the good news! Just by intending to be more intuitive and work with yours allows you to open up to your intuition. Remember, believing that you are intuitive gives your intuition more power. You may notice your feelings more, whether they are physical or emotional. Do you suddenly feel uneasy? Perhaps it's your intuition telling you to watch out.

The problem is, what you receive in this second step are bits and pieces of information that come to you randomly. You're confused and frustrated because you don't know what your intuition is telling you. This is because you don't know the mechanics of how intuition works. This is where most people give up learning how to use their intuition. They never get through Step 2 because they don't practice a technique, or they haven't learned one.

STEP 3 *Intermediate Intuition. You try to find ways to learn about intuition. You learn techniques and methods to develop your intuition and practice.*

If you can get yourself past the initial frustration of experiencing elusive and vague messages of intuition, you will get to move on to Step 3 and search for ways to learn how to strengthen your intuition. You'll discover that, like any skill, you need a technique and methods to apply to intuition to get it to become more reliable, accurate and consistent. Many people then start to seek out books and courses to take to learn some techniques. This is where you come in because you're reading this book!

In this step, you begin to have a format where you can get more intuitive information through understanding the characteristics of intuition, learning a process that allows you to engage with your intuition and intuition exercises to practice. Methods and techniques, also known as tools, give you control over your intuition. Along with understanding how intuition works in the brain and body, you can then make sense of the pieces. You can also control your intuition. Finally, you will become more aware of intuitive messages when they appear and know when it's real or not. One major intuition technique you'll learn about is, "The Intuition On Demand Technique."

With this technique, you'll learn a stepwise process that will trigger your intuition into giving you information on what you want, then as you work with the technique you'll learn how to gain more clarity about your intuitive messages and finally interpret your intuitive messages to give you clear useful guidance.

You certainly can learn other techniques, methods and tools from other teachers and books as well.

STEP 4 *Advanced Intuition. You practice your techniques and methods and hone your intuitive skills as your abilities increase.*

Once you've learned an intuition technique you then need to practice using it. This is Step 4 where you are becoming more successful using your intuition but you are still honing your skills, as your abilities increase. As you build your skill you begin to receive more detailed information as you recognize your intuitive messages and symbols more easily. The technique assists in gathering intuition pieces for you, which builds a story or a scene. You begin to receive more structured answers to your questions that come more quickly now.

You may be using tools to help you stay out of your Ego space. You are still practicing, so you don't always get more hits than misses. You are starting to build tolerance for your misses knowing that your practicing is just that, practice. It is now that you may experience incremental improvement in your hits. Occasionally you may receive a piece of stunning intuitive information that you never thought you could before. You begin to know what it's like to receive a true intuitive message in terms of what it feels like, how it pops up in your mind, because you have experienced when it worked. This is where it is important to write down the times when your intuition worked. No matter what you receive, big hits or little ones celebrate them but keep practicing and don't give up.

In this step you can practice with your friends and family, if they are open to it. This is also a good time to work in a Development Circle, where you can get together and practice with other like-minded people who want to develop their intuitive skills as well.

STEP 5 *A State of Being. You now have the Intuitive Mind and live the Intuitive Life.*

After lots of practice and then reminding yourself constantly that you can use your intuition for all kinds of situations and decisions during your day you begin to live, what I call, an "Intuitive Life." This is the last step on the path. Your intuition is loud and clear to you all the time, and you recognize and notice when it's sending you messages. It is clearer to you when it is your intuition, versus when you're making it up. To others you seem "psychic." Sometimes people say to you, "How did you know that?" At this step, intuitive messages just come when you don't expect it and you no longer have to trigger your intuition to happen. Being highly intuitive all comes naturally to you. Sometimes the messages are big and important, other times they are small and just give you information.

One day I was going to a local organic health food store to buy sushi for lunch. The sushi was in a refrigerated deli section at the back of the store amongst a large selection of organic freshly made pasta and fruit salads, bursting burritos and a multitude of yummy wraps. Walking straight past the salad bar to the deli counter, I saw a woman dressed in business attire walking and talking with a colleague. They were obviously on their lunch break. She seemed very agitated, talking loudly about someone or something that she was in conflict with. As I stood in front of the refrigerated display case I looked over the sushi selections, and Ms. Loud Agitated Lady walked up and stood next to me scanning over the lunch selections.

I used my intuition as I usually do, to allow myself to be drawn to what looked good and was right for me to eat at this time. My intuitive eye immediately was attracted to some salmon sushi, and just before my hand was about to reach for it, Ms. Loud Agitated Lady shot out her's and grabbed it first. A bit irritated and disappointed, I thought to myself, "Aw, I wanted that one." Then my intuition popped in my head clearly saying simply, "She's going to put it back." So I waited as she held it. Then she put it back. And I grabbed it.

That is how your intuition becomes "turned on" all the time, or rather you're tuned in to it all the time to be listening and aware of any messages it's sending you. You are now in a "state of being" where you are receptive all the time. Your psychic senses are on when you need them whether you are aware of it or not.

At this step when you do trigger your intuition, the intuitive answers you receive are complete with more detail. You can ask your intuition anything you want and you will receive in-depth information. The technique that you have practiced is now second nature.

There are lots of stories about people who are saints that have extraordinary psychic abilities. Both Eastern and Western religions have stories of their enlightened saints being connected to divine intuitive knowledge. This is the path of where we all can be in this lifetime. Perhaps you don't become a saint, but you will and can be more aware of "All That Is," God, and Your Creator and connected to the Universe. That is the enlightened intuitive life!

Why People Get Stuck in Step 1 of the Intuition Learning Path

Most people get stuck in Step 1 or Step 2. It's important to know what your obstacles may be so when you run into them, you can get past them. I don't want you to get stuck. There are a few reasons why people get stuck. Let's find out why.

Everyone has been in Step 1, where you've experienced your intuition working at some point in your life. Everyone has intuition and it is always working for you, though you may not have recognized it. So we all start at Step 1. Here are some reasons why people get stuck in Step 1. Some people recognize their intuition as a gut feeling or a knowing and believe their intuition is just a random event. Some people deny their intuition's existence and say it was just coincidence. Just as I used to think, others say they are not intuitive at all because they didn't recognize what intuition was truly like and when their intuition was actually working for them. Many times, if you don't think you are intuitive it is because you haven't been aware of the messages it has been sending you.

Some people are afraid of finding out something scary so they give up. You won't receive scary information from your intuition. That's not the nature of intuition because the messages are never shocking, upsetting or scary. Intuitive messages are generally neutral in tone, and are often in the form of guidance. Your intuition will just tell you, "Stop here now." It will never scream at you something like, *"YOU'RE IN BIG TROUBLE. WATCH OUT, YOU'RE HEADED FOR A HORRIBLE, DANGEROUS, CATASTROPHE! DON'T GO DOWN THAT ROAD, IT'S WASHED OUT AND YOU'LL DROWN!"*

Intuition is always calm, neutral, and comes in a way that is not frightening. If it seems like your intuition is trying to scare you, it is *NOT* your intuition.

You may resist learning about your intuition because you think you can't be intuitive, that it is a gift that only gifted people have. As mentioned earlier, everyone is intuitive, there are no exceptions.

I've found Step 2 is where many of my students are when they come to me to learn about intuition. In Step 2, those people whose interest is now peaked about their intuitive experiences, want to see if they can use their intuition and get more useful information from it. The problem is they didn't have a clear technique to use. Without a proper technique you are just stabbing in the dark, so to speak, because you don't know how to get your intuition to happen when you want. Many times people just wait for their intuition to just do something, and they wait a long time. This is because they don't have a process to access their intuition or understand its characteristics, its language or how to work with the intuitive information they receive.

You may be trying to understand your intuition but it doesn't make sense to you. You may think that your intuition is 'broken' because you're not getting the amazing results you think other people do. Another big reason people give up on their intuition and say it doesn't work is because they try to use their intuition on big important decisions or situations, and they fail. This is like skiing down the advanced level trail when you really need to be on the beginner trail, or perhaps even on the "Bunny slope." Don't try to run before you can walk. Don't give up on your intuition, you *can* do this and become highly intuitive!

The biggest challenge will be to resist trying to figure out what your first intuitive piece means. Often, when you ask your intuition a question, the first intuitive message you receive won't make sense. There is a tendency to then try to figure it out by thinking too much about what that first intuition piece can mean, which usually leads to the wrong answer. This is again where people give up. These are important ways to solve the most frequent problems students have. They often get tripped up with their first intuitive piece especially during an intuition exercise. I will elaborate more on this in the section on how to do intuition exercises.

Here are some Golden Rules so you don't get stuck at the beginning of developing your intuition:

1. *Don't give up before you try. Give yourself a chance to build your skill.*
2. *Don't look for or expect a particular answer you want your intuition to tell you.*
3. *Do not try to deduce or figure out what your first intuition pieces mean.*
4. *You get what you get and you don't get upset.*
5. *Learn a good intuition technique then keep practicing it!*

The Intuitive Life - Learning How to Think Intuitively

It's easy to forget to use your intuition all the time. You're not used to it. I wasn't used to using my intuition in my daily life. I had to remember that I could use it and situations often arose that allowed me to practice using my intuition. You're always making decisions, mostly small ones, which is a great opportunity to use your intuition.

As you work through the techniques and tools in this book, remember that you can practice anytime and when you become highly skilled use your intuition in all aspects of your life. You can use your intuition to make small decisions from which head of lettuce to buy from the stack at the grocery store, to choosing a doctor or specialist for your health issues.

You are on a great adventure to becoming highly intuitive. Your life will change when you reach that advanced level because you will have the comfort of having dependable internal guidance, a message or grace from God letting you know things will be okay, that you are not alone and have assurances of the right thing to do next. It's all very exciting! But first you need to learn an intuition technique and that's what the next chapter is about.

Highlighted Tips and Summary

5 Steps on the Map of the Intuition Learning Path

STEP 1 *"In the Beginning." Intuition has caught your attention but seems random and uncontrollable.*

STEP 2 *Beginner's Intuition. You try to pay attention to your intuition and figure out its messages but you don't understand them.*

STEP 3 *Intermediate Intuition. You try to find ways to learn about intuition. You learn techniques and methods to develop your intuition and practice.*

STEP 4 *Advanced Intuition. You practice your techniques and methods and hone your intuitive skills as your abilities increase.*

STEP 5 *A State of Being. You now have the Intuitive Mind and live the Intuitive Life.*

PART TWO

The Intuition On Demand Technique

CHAPTER 4

Getting Your Intuition Under Your Control: The "Intuition On Demand" Technique

• • • • • • • • • • • • •

Intuition that is out of control and happens once in a while can be very challenging. Even when your intuition is right on for small things, such as intuitively knowing your boss is going to wear a pink shirt that day, but you can't make your intuition help you choose the right job, can really be frustrating. You may find your intuition happens inconsistently, it seems vague or you don't trust it. You may often feel intuition happens "to" you rather than you directing it. A frequent complaint I hear is, "My intuition seems to be random, how do I make my intuition happen when I want?" or "I had a feeling my intuition was telling me something but I didn't know what it meant." Another common complaint is, "I've had lots of times when I should have followed my intuition, but I just didn't trust that it was a real intuitive message."

We have all had a funny feeling about a person or situation, but can't pinpoint what it is, even though we just know our intuition is telling us something. So we shrug it off as us just making it up, and later we find out our feelings were right. It's a natural desire to use that intuition at will and on demand for other situations you find yourself in, but it just doesn't happen for you. To develop intuition control you need a process and technique that works consistently and reliably any time you need it, and be able to get more detailed and useful intuitive information. Most importantly, you'll need a method to know when it's a real intuitive message you can trust.

The Intuition On Demand Technique is a method I developed that works again and again not only for myself, but also for the hundreds of students I've taught. I'll explain why each step in the technique is important, how the steps in the process connect together and solves the following problems with intuition: how to make your intuition happen when you want, on what you want, how to trust it and finally how to get detailed information that is useful. The following chapters will go more deeply into each of the steps to give you examples and methods to use this technique effectively for any situation.

Why a Clear Technique Is Important
for Accuracy and Consistency

Just like any skill you develop, you need a clear step-by-step technique to get started, grow and then master that skill. Whether it be a sport like tennis or golf, learning how to drive a car, or developing your intuition, using techniques and methods helps you learn how to get control over what you are doing and get the results you want. Having steps that are tangible will help you repeat, practice the process, and give you the experience of what it feels like when it works and when it doesn't so you can improve. Without a step-by-step process you're just "stabbing in the dark" at trying to produce results.

You need to master your intuition skills and to do this you need a technique that you can repeat and practice over and over again to improve your skill and gain accuracy and consistency. Eventually you become a master and you no longer remember the steps, it becomes second nature. But to start, it is important that the technique you use has clear and tangible steps that you can follow.

The Secret Behind the Technique

As I mentioned earlier, I did not start out highly intuitive. I didn't consider myself psychic and certainly did not "see spirits" at a young age. In fact, I considered myself non-intuitive. They say everyone has the ability to improve their intuition and I very much wanted to be highly intuitive. So, I began to learn intuition development from scratch.

Psychic development courses focused on the "five psychic senses" and named them the "Clairs," such as clairaudience, which was receiving messages through sound or hearing, which explained how intuition is received but not how to make intuition happen when you wanted it to. The result was that I would sit and wait for an intuitive message to appear through my psychic senses. I sat for a long time just waiting for one to show up. This made the process of trying to deliberately use my intuition quite drawn-out and exasperating.

I then discovered that by closely watching other expert psychics and mediums as they did their readings, they all seemed to go through a process to get intuitive messages for their audience. Some psychic mediums, such as John Holland, speak out loud as they go through their process, talking to their spirit guides along the way.

This observation of their process helped me tremendously. In this way, I began to discover some hidden gems not found in books. I noticed they would constantly ask their guides for help using questions, "Go back over and find out more for me," or "Why are you showing me so and so?" Coupling this with the knowledge I gained from the thousands of hours of study in intuition and psychic development, and energy healing, a highly intuitive process, I began to find overlapping patterns and consistencies on how to work with intuitive information. I also discovered simple ways to shift one's attention to be most open to the intuitive side of the mind. Surprisingly, that mind shift of being open is something we do all the time during our day, but the revelation was how to do it at will and spontaneously.

By putting together all my own experimenting with intuition, experience with successes (and failures) during hundreds of readings, my learned knowledge, observing others and reading scientific research, I created an intuition technique that worked consistently, reliably, and produced results when I wanted it to. This was the secret to the technique: finding what worked for other highly skilled intuitives and myself both in theory and empirically that made intuition easily accessible, clear and tangible.

To my surprise I became a sold out reader at public events. People would have to sign up early in the day for a reading or they couldn't get on my schedule, and some asked me to extend my hours to squeeze in more readings. It was very exciting because the technique worked and then I wanted to share what I knew with others. I now no longer do readings for other people because I would rather teach them to take advantage of this technique to tap into their own intuition and get the messages for themselves.

The Intuition On Demand Technique Overview

The Intuition On Demand Technique is a 5 simple step process that can be used in a variety of situations for different kinds of purposes. The final step reminds you to keep working at it through practice. The 5 steps are, Ask a Question, Be Open, Collect and Receive, Do it Again, Practice. The steps can be conveniently memorized as: A, B, C, D, + P.

A = Ask a Question
B = Be Open
C = Collect and Receive
D = Do it again
P = Practice, practice, practice!

The steps can be visualized as a cycle of question and answer that you practice using. The following figure shows the technique as a cycle of steps.

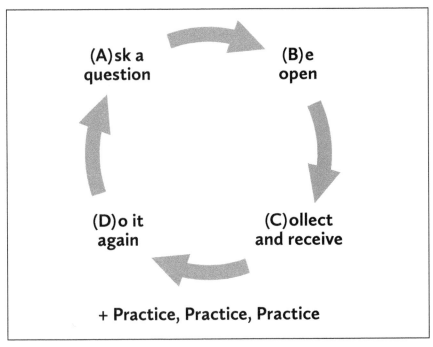

The Intuition On Demand Technique

The basic process of the technique contains all the elements you need and we will go over each step to explain how. The rest of the development of your intuition relies on the variety of questions and ways to trigger your intuition, and then how to practice being open since this is where we trip up. Repeating the process will collect the pieces of information intuition is sending you so you can eventually see the entire message. As your intuition development progresses, you'll learn and experience all the different ways you can receive intuitive information and you will find it can come to you in those different ways, simultaneously, and in combinations. Practicing various exercises hones your intuitive skill to become faster and more specific and detailed.

Here is an overview of the technique and each step:

A – Ask a Question –
Trigger Your Intuition on What You Want

Intuition will always respond to stimuli. The stimulus can be anything, like a thought or something external such as changing our surroundings by turning the corner walking down the street; it might be unseen metaphysical energy or come from inner guidance sending us information. The stimulus can also be simply asking your intuition a question. This allows you to willingly make your intuition happen. Your intuition will always respond as part of your mind reacting to a question and you will always get an intuitive response because you are always thinking, feeling, seeing, hearing, etc. That's the good news about making your intuition happen when you want.

The more difficult part is, by asking a question your thinking and judging part of your mind will reply as well. The key is to ask the right kind of questions, use the right kinds of stimuli that will give your intuition an opportunity to respond more loudly than your thinking mind. Having a set of different ways to present a variety of questions to your intuition is what I call your intuition tool kit. We will go more in depth into the tool kit in the next chapter. Once you trigger your intuition with a question you need to Be Open, which is the next step in the technique.

B – Be Open –
Learn How to Make Your Intuition Consistent

Your thinking mind and Ego get in the way of your intuition by corrupting the true intuitive message, or drowning the message out with non-intuitive thoughts. You then believe your intuition is unreliable and inconsistent because the true intuitive message was lost in the thought confusion. To avoid this, you have to quiet your thinking mind, but you don't have to be in a special state of mind, that is, you are not going into meditation to do it. You are just "being open."

When you are able to be in this open state of mind after you trigger your intuition with a question, you'll be able to receive consistently and clearly what your intuition is telling you. You may find this is one of the more troublesome steps as people often have lots of questions about it. More detail of this step and those questions will be answered in the chapter *How to Make Your Intuition Reliable and Consistent: (B)e Open is the Secret.* Once you're open and ready to receive, you'll need to know what intuitive messages are like so you can recognize them. This leads us to the next step, which is Collect and Receive.

C – Collect Messages –
Know What Real Intuitive Messages Are Like

The third step in the technique is to receive and collect your intuitive messages. It is very important that you know how your intuition comes to you so you know when it is truly an intuitive message. Intuition is the language of the intuitive part of your brain, which "speaks" in pieces of images, a word or two, sounds, thoughts, feelings, and symbols. More importantly, this intuition language presents information in a way that is different from your thinking mind. Intuition does not present messages in a sequential pattern. There is no beginning, then a middle and end in the message. Sometimes the messages are holistic and are given all at once.

Recognizing the characteristics of intuitive messages is also key to distinguishing them from your thinking and judging mind. This is how you begin to know whether it is a real intuitive message or you're just making it up. Intuition characteristics and how to distinguish real intuition from your thinking mind will be discussed in depth in the chapter *How To Know You're Not Making It Up: (C)ollect and Receive Real Intuition Messages.* As you go through this process you will be collecting intuitive messages that pop up at you. They will often be fragments and pieces of the message. These are the pieces of information that you accumulate through the Q&A cycle, which is the next step.

D – Do It Again

The next step in this technique is to Do It Again. This means you are going to repeat the first three steps, Ask a Question, Be Open and Collect and Receive again which will give you more intuitive pieces of information. By doing these 3 steps over and over, you collect and get detail about what your intuition is telling you. Intuition speaks in symbols, signs, and in fragments and pieces. When you initially work as a beginner with your intuition, you often only receive or notice one piece at a time. One piece of the puzzle is confusing and unclear. You have to go back and get more pieces. As you collect more pieces eventually they will form a complete message that will make more sense to you.

The technique of asking a question, being open and collecting your answers is very powerful to find out the entire message that your intuition is passing to you. The next most important thing to do is to practice the technique so it works effortlessly for you and get to the point where you don't even realize you are asking questions. Your mind will automatically connect and collect intuitive messages on things you want to know about. The best way to practice is to do intuition exercises.

P – Practice

The last step in the Intuition On Demand Technique is to practice the technique as often as you can. As you know, practice makes perfect, or in this case, practicing your intuition exercises hones your intuition so you will get more detail and receive intuitive information faster. An important aspect to practicing with your intuition is to select good exercises for intuition and know how to practice properly. Ideally, you should practice with a partner, that is, someone who is of like mind and interested in helping you or interested in improving their intuition so you can change roles during your exercises. Again, there is a right way and a wrong way to do intuition exercises and this will be explained in a later chapter. Also, later in the book, there will be many great intuition exercises you can do at home or with a partner.

In the next chapters, I will show you how to use this technique in detail, where and when to use it and how it works in different scenarios and situations. It is important to keep the overall 5-Step Intuition Technique in mind because you will be using it over and over again in a variety of ways. You will always go back to it as we expand and explain each step.

Highlighted Tips and Summary

The Intuition On Demand Technique:

A = Ask a Question
B = Be Open
C = Collect and Receive
D = Do it again
P = Practice, practice, practice!

CHAPTER 5

How to Make Your Intuition Happen When You Want, on What You Want: (A)sk a Question

• • • • • • • • • • • • •

Before studying intuition development I only had two vivid intuitive experiences that I remember. The first one happened in my college days while I was asleep, the other experience was with my Dad as I already told you about in the beginning of the book. It was this second experience that convinced me that intuition inexplicably works. As I mentioned, dreaming is a common time when people receive intuitive information. For me, my dream was telling me a friend was in trouble.

Earlier that evening, I was out having a late pizza dinner with some friends, David, Steven and Sandy. Steven and Sandy were a couple. The food and drinks were good, and we all were having a great time even though it was the end of a long day for me and I was very tired. We soon split up to go home. I was exhausted and needed to go to bed. I was feeling the kind of tired where the moment your head hits the pillow you're asleep.

The moment I began to drift to sleep I started dreaming about Steven who, in my dream, was very upset and arguing with me. The dream was so vivid it briefly woke me up. I rolled over and fell asleep again. This happened a couple of times when the last dream became more detailed. This time Steven was still arguing and pleading, this time begging for me to do something. I could see and feel but I couldn't hear anything. In the dream, I knew I couldn't do what he asked. We were standing in a stairwell, he looked down at me from two stairs up and was sobbing, tears running down his red cheeks, his arms animated. I heard no words, his mouth moved in silence. As I dreamt, I had the feelings of telling him I just couldn't do what he was begging me to do. At the same time my heart was torn, I felt so strongly that I didn't want him hurting but not knowing what else to say, I just couldn't agree with him. I woke up again, frustrated that I couldn't fall into the deep sleep my body wanted.

Then the phone rang. Shocked, I grabbed it and all I could say was, "YES??" It was David. He said he had been texting with Steven for the past hour and was very worried about him. Steven was very despondent and said Sandy just broke up with him. She told him right after our dinner. She couldn't be with him any longer, she said, it's been too long and too hard. She'd made her decision. He was devastated and distraught.

Apparently, Steven was somewhere on campus finishing a six-pack of beer, and definitely not in a stable frame of mind. His last texts said he couldn't go on without her, that he was going to end it all. David said he didn't know what to do, he tried to call Steven and text him but there was no response. Neither of us was on campus at the time. We were both very worried about Steven and felt someone needed to help him. I told David to call the on-call Student Dean and explain the conversation. That put a quick search into action and Steven was found before he got into any trouble and was given assistance.

The next day, I spoke to Sandy, who was obviously very upset and concerned. She was the one who alerted David first that night and asked him for help. She was afraid of Steven's state of mind as well. She felt awful when she told Steven she was breaking up with him and he fell to pieces. He pleaded with her to stay with him. She said, unlike many other times where she'd go back to him, this time she just couldn't. It then dawned on me that their conversation was in my dream. So I asked her, "Were you in a stairwell when you were talking to him?" She said, "Yes." I asked, "Was the stairwell grey with a dark grey railing?" She looked a bit startled and said, "Yes." I pressed further, "Was he standing two steps above you when you were talking?" Her eyes widened and she said, "Yes! Oh my God! How did you know that??"

I told her, "I saw him in my dream. I was dreaming that he was pleading with me about something, crying and standing in a stairwell two steps above me." I started to realize that I was seeing it through her eyes even though I was in my bed 20 miles away.

That insightful, intuitive, psychic experience was so shocking to me I wouldn't have believed it unless I went through it myself. Wouldn't it be great if I could harness that intuition power on other things? The problem was, it seemed to happen when I was asleep. How do I get my intuition to work for me when I was awake? My intuition seemed to only work randomly.

Why Is Your Intuition Random?

Intuition was not under your control because you didn't know how to make it happen. I also waited for my intuition to appear. I waited in my dreams, while I was standing on line at the grocery store, when I first met someone new. I waited for a long time and nothing happened.

You want to use your intuition on what you want and when you want it. But, it doesn't happen for you that way. Your intuition may be a vague experience. You may feel you don't have control over it, and often, you may not even know if your intuition is working or happening at all. When your intuition was right, you only know it after the fact. You say to yourself, "I had a feeling that was going to happen." Perhaps, like me, you feel like intuition happens to you rather than being able to use your intuition when you want it to.

Now I'll give you the solution as Step 1 of the Intuition On Demand Technique. This is what you must do to get your intuition to act. You trigger your intuition by asking it a question.

Start by Setting Your Intention

It is always good to do a preparation step of "Setting Your Intention." If you are asking your intuition a question, it's good to keep in mind that your intuition is the way you receive, what I like to believe is, divine guidance. That guidance can come from your angels, guides, or your higher self. Perhaps it is coming from the wiser part of you that your judging, fearful, doubtful mind is drowning out.

An intention is as simple as declaring to yourself that you are going to ask help from divine consciousness, or wherever you would like to receive guidance from. I personally love angels and often ask to receive messages from them through my intuition. You can set a general intention to receive messages intuitively from divine guidance, that Universal Consciousness is the One in all of us. Our thoughts are very powerful and our intentions have even more energy behind them. You can ask for the highest most loving and powerful thing that you believe in to help you and give you messages through your intuition.

Setting an intention is easy when done through a prayer. You don't have to be religious or follow any particular religion. An intention that I was taught to say before doing an intuitive reading is, "I now ask for your angels and guides and my angels and guides to come now to give you messages for your highest good." You can use that too if you like it. If you don't want to pray then you can just have an intention to receive messages for your highest good from divine sources.

Your "highest good" is an awesome thing because you don't have to be specific about what you are asking for. This allows you to set an intention for what you had in mind or something better that is for your highest good. A friend of mine, Anne Marie, always says that you should, "Ask for this or something better." We don't always know what the best is for us, so your intention can request from divine wisdom, God, source, your angels or guides, that they give you what is best for you.

Now that you have set your intention to receive messages and information from the highest, best sources for your highest good you are now ready to engage your intuition.

How to Ask Your Intuition a Question

Now you are ready to get your intuition to work for you on demand. You do this by triggering your intuition to act by asking it a question. It's important to understand that you are not asking yourself the question, but you are asking your intuition as if it were not YOU. You are not asking yourself the question, because the thinking mind identifies with "yourself." The thinking mind, when asked a question, will automatically try to come up with an answer. Your intuition will answer as well, but your intuition is quieter than your thinking mind and you won't hear her if they are both talking at once. This is why it is important that you should ask your intuition a question as if it isn't *YOU*.

There is a reason for this. In essence, there are many systems in your brain that you are both conscious and not conscious of. Some of these systems are what make up your intuitive mind, which you're not always conscious of. It is almost as if you have a separate part of "you" that is picking up messages and information, processing and making sense of it, but you are unaware of it. This is the intuitive side of you or your intuitive mind. A later chapter will explain how this works in the brain.

You trigger your intuition by asking a question that you pose silently in your mind. You can ask your intuition a question out loud but it's not necessary. If you're not used to asking questions to yourself, or "talking" to yourself, you can practice! No one needs to know you're doing it since you're just asking a question in your mind. The good thing about this part of the technique is no one needs to know that you're talking to your intuition. You'll be asking your intuition a lot of questions silently, so get yourself used to it.

Asking Your Intuition the Right Kinds of Questions

There are good questions and bad questions to ask your intuition. Good questions keep your thinking mind guessing and slow to respond, which gives your intuition a chance to answer fast and be heard. Your intuition will always answer and respond quickly, so you don't have to wait for it to answer. Again, the trick is not letting your thinking mind get in the way. That's where asking the right question is important. I'll give you some examples to help clarify. First let's start with the kinds of questions that are bad, or not so good, to ask your intuition.

Bad Questions

Generally, questions that are not good to ask your intuition are: "yes or no" questions, questions that are rhetorical, and highly emotional questions.

"Yes or no" questions are questions that have a "yes" or "no" answer. These are not good questions to ask because it's too easy for your thinking mind to jump in and answer yes or no. Here are some examples of yes or no questions that are not good: "Should I take this job offer?" or "Is he my soul mate?"

Rhetorical questions are not good questions to ask your intuition. Rhetorical questions are, by definition, questions that are not expected to be answered so they are not good to ask your intuition. For example, "I'm beautiful, aren't I?" This also goes for questions that you think you already know the answer to, or more importantly, that you want a particular answer for. The biggest pitfall for messing up receiving true intuition is anticipating and looking for an answer you want from your intuition. To combat this, you can ask an indirect question or use intuition tools, which we'll go over in the next chapter.

There are also times when it is not good for you to ask your intuition a question. When is not a good time to ask? When you are extremely emotionally upset or when your mind is not clear. If this is the case, then you can wait until you are a little calmer and have a clearer mind. Also, asking questions that are highly charged with emotion are not good questions to ask your intuition either. Your emotions get in the way of your ability to recognize a true intuitive message. For example, this would be a bad emotional question to ask your intuition, "*Why does my ex-boyfriend hate me?*" A better question to ask would be, "*What can I do to improve my next relationship?*"

Good Questions to Ask

Good questions to ask your intuition are ones that are emotionally neutral and are open-ended. An open-ended question is one that cannot be answered with a one-word answer such as yes or no. Open-ended questions require your thinking mind to give it some thought before answering and usually the thinking mind gives an answer that is wordy. That takes time for your thinking mind to come up with an answer, but for your intuition, it will answer immediately. In essence, you are stalling your thinking mind a bit and this gives your intuition an opportunity to quickly respond and be recognized.

Here are examples of good questions to ask your intuition:

Open-ended questions, such as, "What can I do to get more customers for my business?" "What can I do to change the way my boyfriend treats me?" Some non-emotional examples would be, "What will be the health status of my mom 3 weeks from now?" "Who are the people that affect my reputation the most at work and how?"

General questions can be good when you don't know what to ask – "Give me a message for my highest good."

Here are some other examples of good questions to exercise your intuition:

- "*Which way is the car in front of me going to go, where will they exit?*"
- "*Which line at the grocery store is fastest?*"
- "*What time will my subway train arrive at the station?*"
- "*What time will the doctor call me in?*"

Highlighted Tips and Summary

The first step in the Intuition On Demand Technique is, *Ask a Question.* Our minds, and brain will always react to a stimulus, which in this case is a question. Ask the right kinds of questions – open ended and questions that do not have "yes" or "no" as the answer.

CHAPTER 6

Your Intuition Toolkit – 10 Intuition Tools

• • • • • • • • • • • • •

The Intuition Toolkit is a group of techniques that are shortcuts to work with your intuition. These are refined tools and methods to help present a "problem" to your intuition so it can answer with useful information. These are methods that I have collected, discovered and created which have been shown to work time and time again to provide quick results. When you don't have a tool to work with, you may find yourself waiting for your intuition to appear with a message. Your intuition may be giving you a message but it's not very clear and you end up missing it. A tool will help bridge the gap between a vague intuition message and clear information. Your intuition can give you a message through the tool plus you have the tool to pay attention to, so now you're both in the same place. Intuition tools combined with asking your intuition a question make a powerful way to trigger your intuition into action. Without the tools you can find yourself stuck, and with a tool you can get past your intuition blocks, such as thinking or doubt, and more easily get a true intuitive message.

The toughest part of working with your intuition will be getting your Ego and thinking mind out of the way of receiving your intuitive messages. These tools are designed to prevent the cross talk of your thinking mind drowning out your intuitive mind. Intuition Tools are just that, they are only tools to help you get a desired result. The intuitive messages are not in the tools themselves. The tools give your intuitive mind something to use to communicate more easily with you. It is the best way to get out of your "Ego space" since your Ego is 100% non-intuitive.

Intuition Tools are good to use when you are in an emotionally charged situation and you want to use your intuition to get help with making decisions or to find out more information. The following tool list is laid out with a description of the tool first, then generally how it is used, then a step-by-step process of using it. Intuition Tools are a powerful way to access your intuition directly to get messages quickly and easily in any situation. *Keep in mind that each tool will use the Intuition On Demand technique, where you go through the cycle of question and answer, but using the tool as a focal point.*

1. Using a Person's First Name

You can receive intuitive information about someone from just his or her first name. This tool is very powerful. You can use this method when gathering intuitive information about a situation that involves people. You might be asking how is this possible if several people have the same name? Since everything is energy and connected to that energy, including thoughts, physical things and our soul or spirit essence, we are also connected to all things that are related to us. This includes our name. While you may have the same first name as someone else, the energy vibration associated with you using your own name is uniquely connected to you. Your name holds energy that best suits your life purpose for this incarnation. It is that energy that we are intuitively picking up.

Your parents were guided to give you this name, and if they ignored this guidance you may go through life feeling that your name doesn't fit you. This is why people often have nicknames or may want to change their name. Also, if you are doing an intuitive reading for someone, your sitter is usually connected to the person whose name they are giving you. Otherwise, they wouldn't be sharing it with you. It may be the name of their relative, boss, co-worker, friend, or significant other. That connection also has an energetic link to the person whose name it is. All of this energy that is connected to the name is what you are picking up. It's almost like a road map to the named person and also carries information about them. You can also intuitively pick up if the named person uses a nickname, and you may find their nickname or the name they most often use has a strong energetic vibration. This means when you use the name they use most often, you'll get more information from that name that are hits. You don't need a last name, though sometimes last names do add more energetic information.

HOW

Here are different ways you can use this Name tool. Say you just started a new job and you're given the name of your new boss but you haven't met them yet. You can use this tool to find out more about them intuitively. Or perhaps you are going out on a blind date and you only know the name of your date. Using the first name, you can now ask your intuition questions about the person. You can try this for yourself right now. Pick someone you know and think of his or her first name. See what impressions you get. What feelings, thoughts or impressions come up when you think of this person's name? This is how you will receive intuitive information from someone's name. Here is how you use this tool.

STEP-BY-STEP

1. Write the person's name on a piece of paper and then put your attention on the name. Ask your intuition the question, "What can you tell me about this person?"
2. Be open to receiving what you feel, see, hear, about the person in your mind, or perhaps what thoughts pop up about them. Even though you may have known many people by the same name, as you tune in, you may receive a feeling about the person's personality and character right away. You may get a feeling, or an image or an understanding of the person and it often comes up quickly.
3. Write down what comes up first. As you receive information, you may get more and more or it may come in little spurts. Keep writing what you receive. Do not edit anything.

As you pick up information intuitively, you may get a feeling that the name doesn't quite fit and you may feel like a nickname or a shortened version feels better. For example, I once was reading for someone who was starting to see a person named Martin. I wrote his name down on a piece of paper. As I tuned into his name, I felt he was a strong person, both personality wise and physically, which I explained to her. I then felt that Martin didn't quite feel right, that his name didn't fit his personality at all. I felt that people didn't call him Martin because he didn't like it, and used a shortened version, or a very different nickname. "That's right, but his nickname wasn't even Marty, it was an unusual nickname," she said, "No one ever calls him Martin."

You can write the name down on a piece of paper and allow your pen or pencil to write whatever doodles it wants to around the name. You may find yourself underlining the name or drawing shapes around the name unconsciously. Here's a good example. One time I drew a box around someone's name and I received that the person felt boxed in, which the client said was correct.

You may also get impressions from the name of someone else that you know with the same name. This is fine. Your intuition may be bringing up that person because the name of the target person you're trying to get information about may have similarities with them. When you write down what you get intuitively, don't edit anything you've written because you may be surprised at the results.

Once you have a first name you can ask your intuition the following kinds of additional questions to trigger it to respond. These are examples, but you can come up with more on your own. Let's say the first name is "Harry." You can ask:

- "What do I need to know about *HARRY?*"
- "What kind of personality does *HARRY* have?"
- "What are *HARRY's* likes and dislikes?"
- "What does *HARRY* look like?"
- "Where does *HARRY* live?"

Be open to receiving your intuitive pop-ups. Write everything down, do not edit or judge what you write, even if you're drawing instead of writing words, or you're writing one word or two instead of sentences.

2. Using a Photograph of Someone

As you may suspect, you can pick up quite a bit of information about a person just by looking at their picture. Your intuition can also be triggered to pick up information from a person's photograph. Your intuition can reveal aspects of their personality from the photograph and more. Some of this might be revealed in the photo, but sometimes not: a smiling person may not be a happy person. Learning how to use a photograph to trigger intuitive information is very useful. When you are more skilled with this, you will no longer need a photograph but can use this tool with people you see around you.

HOW

It is important to start with using a photograph that is best to read intuitively. Best photos to use are where:

- You can see a full face that has been lit with decent lighting.
- You don't need to see the entire body in the picture, but a face is most important.
- There is no one else in the photograph so you don't have distractions from your Ego.
- It is a casual photograph because they are better than those that are too posed.
- You can use a physical photo, or a photograph on a phone, tablet or computer.

A photograph of a person will trigger your intuition and give you intuitive impressions and pop-ups. You can write these down as you receive them. One more thing, if you want to do this as an exercise with someone else, the best photographs are of a person they know well. This is because if they use a photograph of someone they don't know well, they cannot validate the information that you receive intuitively. As mentioned, only have one person in the photograph with a clear view of their face. You can take the photograph in your hand and look at the person's face carefully. You'll receive intuitive insight often by where your eye is drawn to look at. You can then ask your intuition questions about what you are seeing.

STEP-BY-STEP

1. Take the photograph of the person being read and focus on the person in the picture.
2. Ask your guides and angels, "Tell me about this person, what do I need to know about them?"
3. Notice your physical and emotional reactions to this question. You may receive a feeling, a vision, an impression, a thought, or hear something in your mind. You may feel happiness, sadness, warmth or coolness. These things tell you about the characteristics of the person in the picture. Do not dismiss anything!!
4. When you look at a photo, pay attention to what you immediately feel from the person's face.

5. Try to empathize with what that person is feeling, what their perspective of the world is.
6. You can ask your intuition these questions:

- How is this person related to the sitter?
- What is this person's personality like?
- Where do they live?
- Is there a message your guides and angels want the sitter to know about this person?

As you receive information and answers *WRITE* them down. Write until you feel there is nothing more to receive. Write what first comes to you and do not edit anything. It may be feelings, or images, write those too. It's important that you don't rationalize what you're looking at, nor be misled by clothing, or others in the photograph.

3. Tools You Can Put in Your Hand - Divination Tools

Divination is defined as using signs, such as an arrangement of tea leaves in a cup, oracle cards such as tarot cards, or even reading the burning embers in a fire, traditionally, to predict the future. Divination tools are also a good way to access your intuitive mind by giving your intuition a way to draw your attention to symbols and signs in the tools that are part of the pop-up message. Your intuition will generally draw your attention or awareness to things around you that have symbolic meaning for what it is trying to communicate to you. This is why everything you see, feel, hear, etc., inside or outside of you is part of your intuitive message.

Some examples of divination tools include looking at lines in the palm of your hand (palmistry), looking into a mirror, bowl of water, or crystal ball (called scrying), looking at the cracks in a turtle's shell, patterns of numbers (numerology) or sticks and stones thrown on the ground. Again, while these are tools, the practical aspect of divination is not the tool itself, but the intuitive guidance we receive while using them. These tools are just to get us out of our Ego space, which is non-psychic. You can use almost anything as a tool.

HOW

There are hundreds of divination tools and methods out there. Generally, the tools create patterns that seem random, but are guided by what is thought to be divine forces. Anything can be used as a tool to receive intuitive messages including a child's memory block set. My son had a set of wooden tiles with a picture on each one as part of a memory game. I realized that these tiles could be grabbed randomly out of a bag and used as a divination tool by looking at the pictures. We used these in an actual classroom of intuition students and they worked quite well!

The reason why divination tools work with your intuition is that everything is energy and that energy is connected to everything. Energy is also consciousness and through working with our conscious intention, intuition and things around us can give us valuable information. This is also how astrology can use the stars to tell us about ourselves! While we are using these tools to help us access its information, it is our intuition that works with that energy to receive the message.

Most divination systems have a "key" which is a reference guide to help you interpret the symbols, but most of the systems rely on intuition for interpretation. The symbols can be a pattern of numbers, images that are drawn on items such as a stone, or made from a set of cards drawn from a deck. These patterns then are matched to their meaning in the reference guide. For example, a deck of angel cards often has a picture and a few words or sentence on each card. Each of those cards is listed in a booklet that describes the divined meaning of the card. To use these divination tools with your intuition, you allow your intuition to be triggered by the tool to give you a message, rather than look up the message in the reference book.

One of the best tools to use for developing your intuition is oracle cards, and I personally prefer angel oracle cards because they generally don't have frightening images on them. For illustrative purposes of how to use a divination tool, we'll go over using angel oracle cards here. You can purchase a deck of angel cards from most bookstores or at an online bookstore. I recommend Doreen Virtue's angel card decks because the pictures are beautiful and detailed which is good for triggering your intuition through seeing. Also, there are no scary pictures or words in these cards. Angel oracle cards also attract and connect with the beautiful metaphysical energy of the angels. Your intuition will then transmit a message from them to you.

STEP-BY-STEP

1. To purchase a new oracle deck, when you are looking in the store or online, pick the one that you are most attracted to and gives you the best emotional feeling inside. After you've taken your deck home, first open your new deck of cards and consecrate your deck by touching each card and imbuing each card with your energy. You can do this by looking at each card and placing it down on the table, going through each card one by one.

2. If you've used the cards previously, especially if you used them to do an intuitive reading for someone else, clear the cards this way. Hold them in your non-dominant hand that is the hand you don't write with, and give them a wrap with your knuckles with your dominant hand.

3. Begin your intuitive reading by first saying an intention or a prayer over the cards. Fan the cards out with the pictures facing you and place them over your heart then say your intention or prayer. This is an example of one you can use when doing an intuitive angel reading for others: *"I now ask for my angels and spirit guides and your angels and spirit guides to come now and give us a clear message for your highest good. Amen."*

4. Think of a question you want to ask your angels. Then shuffle the cards any way you wish and as you do you can ask the angels a question which will trigger your intuition to respond with a message. If you have a card that "jumps" out as you shuffle, then put that one aside to read later. Then ask your intuition the question that you want to receive messages about. You can ask anything or ask for a general message. You will probably not receive the correct lottery numbers, since there is too much emotional baggage around that question. But you can ask for messages for your highest good.

5. When you hear in your head from your intuition or feel intuitively that you should stop shuffling, then stop shuffling.

6. You can then ask your intuition how many cards to pull and perhaps how to spread them out. You may receive intuitively that it may be 1 or 3 or 5 cards to pull, or any number. For simplicity here, deal out three cards and spread the cards out picture side up in front of you.

7. Your intuition will now respond with pop-up messages by point-ing your attention to different parts of the upturned cards. You can now look at each card. As you read the words on the cards and look at the pictures, you may get intuitive pop-up impressions, feelings, words or concepts in your head. The intuitive message is NOT always in the words, but may be in the picture and some-times you may just receive intuitive messages that are not related to the cards. Everything you receive is part of your intuitive mes-sages. This includes how you feel, what you see, whether it pops up in the cards or not.

8. Sometimes the significance of card placement is chronological order, i.e., past, present, future, and sometimes it is not, you can ask your intuition if this is so. As you look at the cards see what you're drawn to look at. If it is a part of the picture, you can then ask your intuition, "Why are you showing me this part of the picture?" This then triggers your intuition to answer with an-other intuitive piece of information. As you collect the intuition pop-ups a story or bigger meaning may reveal itself to you. You may also see a running theme across the set of cards you drew.

9. The most important thing about any reading is that you have trust and also that you trust what you are receiving. Do not edit what you get. Just keep going back and forth between asking your in-tuition questions about what you are receiving and collecting the intuitive pop-ups by using the Intuition On Demand Technique.

10. Interpreting the intuitive messages from using the cards is not always exactly what you see on the card in the words or even the photos. You have to notice your intuitive pop-ups and not "try" to create a message. Just let it come.

4. Looking Into the Future and the Past – Using a Timeline

One of the most popular reasons people want an intuitive or psychic read-ing is to find out about the future. This tool will help you receive intuitive information about the future or the past. It's important to know that the future is not set in stone and that we all have free will to change it. What you pick up about the future now may be different when the time actually comes. Here's an example of how this can happen.

One evening I was attending a ceremony for initiating people into a sacred circle. We were all to go up individually and there was a woman, Helen, who let us know she would determine the order in which people were going to be lined up in. She would be calling us up one by one but we needed to wait a bit longer as she was still shuffling the order of names around. There were about 30 people in the room. As I waited I thought, "Oh! I can practice using my intuition to predict when I'll be called up." So I asked my intuition where she would place me in the line-up and I received, "First." I was surprised! As I waited a bit longer, I thought, "Really? Am I really going to be first?" I asked my intuition again, "When will I be called up?" But, this time I received, "Last." Wow, okay, I thought, now I received two answers, so I asked again and received the same answer, "Last."

As the ceremony started, I was not called first. Time wore on and one by one people were called up and finally, I found out that I was indeed called last. So, my intuition was right! Being curious now, I nonchalantly spoke to Helen about her picking the lineup saying, "I picked up that you would put me last on the line." Helen replied, "Yes, actually, I was going to put your first, but I later changed my mind, because being last is a very honored place." I realized from this my intuition was giving me correct information all the time and that the future is not set in stone but can change by people's will and intention.

HOW

To use this tool you will imagine a timeline or a clock in your mind. If you want, you can write a timeline down on a piece of paper. A timeline is a graphical depiction of time along a line in terms of time intervals. Those time intervals can be days, months, and years or even hours, you can use whatever you'd like. You will use the timeline to pick up events intuitively. For example, they can be major events that are coming up, like a graduation date, or some other milestones in life. You can write down time events in the future or in the past depending on what times you want to get intuitive information about. If you want to go into the past, you would write time intervals that go into the past. Here is how to do this step by step.

STEP-BY-STEP

1. First draw your timeline on a piece of paper. The easiest may be weeks, months or even years. For example, write down today's

month, say it's January, then next write down February, March, April, and so on. Put down as many names of the months, days, weeks or years as time interval markers that you want to go into the future to get intuitive information about. Remember, you can also go into the past as well and put down as many time markers, i.e., months, days, weeks or years in the past.

2. Then look at your timeline on the paper. Say you want to know about your career's future. You can ask your intuition a question such as, "What will my job and career be like at these marker points?" Look at where you are today on the timeline and then scan down the timeline from marker to marker. Go slowly and allow your intuition to pop-up messages to you by being open.

3. Write down or note in your mind everything that comes to you, do not edit anything. You can ask other questions as well pertaining to your career such as, "When will I change jobs?" or "What will my relationship be like with my boss?"

4. Remember you can also scan backward in time to receive intuitive information about those events in the past. You can also use an analog clock face where instead of hours on the clock you use months or years, then imagine going around the clock as time goes forward. You do not have to write your timeline down, you can imagine it in your mind and move through the timeline in your imagination. You may move your hand through the air as you go from time marker to marker to help you note your place on the timeline while you receive intuitive pop-up pieces.

5. Seeing Where You Have Never Been – Remote Viewing

It is actually possible to see places that you've never been to just by using your intuition. There have been extensive scientific studies on this phenomenon done by the US government with some amazing results. Some of these studies are detailed out in a later chapter called Scientific Studies That Are Literally Mind Blowing.

Remote Viewing is a great intuition exercise when you work with a partner since the intuitive messages can be relatively accurately validated. You may be wondering if we are picking up intuitive information about a place from our partner, who has been there. This may be true, but it is theoretically possible that you can pick up information about any place that no one has been to. Validation can be exciting when your remote viewing turned out to be accurate. A client of mine told me years later that the description I gave her during a reading through remote viewing of her father's house was accurate. She had never seen her father's house before. One day her mother showed her a photograph of the house and my client described the inside of the house to her mom. Her mom was surprised that it was so accurate and said, "But, you've never seen the house before, how did you know?"

My client explained that she had an intuitive reading where I described the house to her. This demonstrates two things about remote viewing. The first is that intuitive information received through remote viewing is easily validated and the second is that the information is not necessarily coming from a person related to the location. In this case, my client did not know herself what her father's house looked like and the remote viewing description was validated later for her.

This is why remote viewing can be a great intuition exercise. It is one of the few things where your intuition can be accurately validated. This is because most people can accurately tell you "yes" or "no" about a place they know on what you think you received intuitively during the exercise. Let's go over how to do remote viewing to receive intuitive information about a place.

HOW

Using your intuition to do remote viewing uses the same intuition technique taught here. You trigger your intuition with a stimulus, which in this case is the location of a place. In this case it may be an address, or a place someone gives you, like his or her home, office, apartment, etc. Asking your intuition to show you this place, you can start with the outside facing the structure, then ask your intuition to take you inside. You can "explore" this way using your intuition to "walk" you through the remote location.

STEP-BY-STEP

1. Trigger your intuition to access information about the remote location by stating an address, the name of the place or some identifying reference, for example, "My grandmother's home in Chicago." If you are doing an intuition exercise with someone else, your exercise partner should give you a specific location, for

example, "My home where I live now." It is even possible to just give latitude and longitude coordinates for a location, but you may want to start with something easier to remember. Your sitter can give you a location if you are practicing with a partner.

2. Close your eyes and ask your intuition to show you this place. Ask your intuition, "What does this place look like?"

3. Imagine you are standing outside in front of this structure or building. Be open and see what your intuition gives you in terms of pop-up images, or feelings or even words. Everything you receive is part of your intuitive message.

4. Here are some things you may want to notice: Colors, structures, what does it look like outside? What do you see around this structure? What does the building look like from your vantage point; are you looking at the front? Notice how big is the structure, for example, how many floors are there?

5. Next step, imagine you are going through the front door and see what your intuition shows you. For example: How many rooms can you see from the foyer? Where are the rooms and what kind of rooms are there? Do you see hallways? Stairways? Where are they? Explore this place in your mind, and if you see a doorway or a hallway ask to go through it and "see" what pops up.

6. Remember your intuition may give you information that is not just through images. You may also intuitively pick things up with your feelings; how does the building feel to you? Is it light, heavy, happy or sad? You may receive intuitive pop-ups that are not only in your mind's eye, but you may hear something or know something about this place.

6. Asking for a Sign

Another tool that is easy to use is to ask for a sign. Looking for signs from divine sources to receive information has been part of human history since antiquity. There are numerous references to signs delivered divinely in religious texts. Even angels appearing to people are certainly considered a heavenly sign. Your intuition is the way your divine messages communicate with you, therefore you can ask your intuition to receive a divine message in the form of a sign.

HOW

Simply ask your intuition for a sign regarding what you want to know about. It's usually reassuring to have a sign knowing that things are okay. Signs can come in many ways and you probably have heard of some. People ask to see white feathers as signs of angels, or pennies or dimes as a sign that a passed loved one is near. Another sign is seeing patterns of numbers.

For me, the number 4 is the number of the angels and I asked my angels to show me the number 44 to let me know when they are around helping me and that they are supporting me. Then I saw the number 44 everywhere. But 44 seemed like it may be more likely to occur than say, 444. So, I asked for my angels to show me 444, which I then saw more frequently. I didn't stop there, I then asked to see 4444! Seeing four 4s in a row is less likely than one 4 or even three 4's. But surprisingly, I started seeing 4444 everywhere on license plates, on signs, in phone numbers, on my computer, etc. This really shows that asking for signs in numbers can work.

Again, you can ask for any kind of sign type, a feather, a coin, a color, or even an unusual sign. John Edward asked to see a blue feather, since blue feathers are unusual and not likely to be found. One day at an event, he was rushing out of the bathroom and ran into a table with books on it. Knocking the books on the ground, when he bent over to pick them up, he saw that each one had a big blue feather on the cover!

STEP-BY-STEP

1. Ask your angels or guides to show you a sign, which will have a meaning that you'd like to give it.
2. Be confident that your intuition will guide you to see the sign.
3. Your intuition will draw your attention to look in certain places or perhaps catch a glimpse of something passing by. Be open to what is around you. Your intuition has a holistic awareness, meaning it sees the big picture; it will nudge you to notice when your guides or angels are displaying a sign for you to see.

One last word: there is a danger of a strong desire to see a sign that can corrupt the message. You don't have to force a sign to be there. Set your intention to see a sign, ask that you do and then let it go. Not everything is a sign, so don't force a meaning onto what seems like one when you have to work hard to make it fit. Signs will be undeniably clear.

7. Scanning Someone's Energy

"What is that psychic energy thing?" is a common question when studying intuition or psychic development. You can intuitively scan someone else's body for "dis-ease" or pain. What you are doing is using your intuition to sense someone's energetic field. The human Aura is the extension of the energetic field that everyone has. This is explained further in a later chapter in this book. You can use this tool to pick up information about the layer of the human energy field that corresponds to a person's physical condition.

The physical manifestation of your body is an expression of your energetic body according to metaphysics. By using your intuition to sense someone's energetic field you can intuitively gain information about the field. In fact, most, if not all, energy healing modalities use intuition as part of their technique to heal. It is important to remember that this is *NOT* a method to diagnose someone's illness. Only doctors can legally do that, and unless you are a doctor, you cannot diagnose physical illnesses. That being said, this method is still just indicating information about someone's energy field.

HOW

There are two ways you can start out using this tool, one is using your hand to pass through someone's energy field, and the other is to use your mind's eye to present a silhouette or outline of a person to your intuition then see what your intuition responds with. In both cases, your intuition is triggered by a stimulus. The first one is your action of passing your hand over someone's body, which is through their energy field. The second is presenting your intuition with an image of their body, in this case it is a silhouette representing them. By experimenting with these methods and practicing them with someone else you can discover how your intuition gives you information from a person's energy field. This is how I discovered mine.

One evening I was attending a demonstration of crystal healing by a woman who had a background in Native American healing practices. She asked if anyone in the audience had back pain and she would demonstrate how to heal it. A tall black-haired gentleman raised his hand in the back of the room, and she selected him to come up. She asked him to just stand in front of her and relax. Then with a large quartz crystal in her hand she began to make large up and down sweeping motions with the crystal over the front of his body. It was a little boring to watch so I thought to myself, "I know, while I'm watching him, I'll see if I can see his aura!" Now, I had never seen an aura before with my physical eyes, and to this day, I still don't. So I relaxed my eyes, and tried to look at him with a soft focus which is what I read helped you see auras. It didn't work. I thought, "I can see it with my mind's eye." I would watch her and then close my eyes, then open them to watch again, back and forth. Each time I closed my eyes, imaging that his outline was standing there in my mind's eye.

My intuition popped a change to the image I had in my mind's eye. The image now had this black-grey fog that seemed to come out of his upper back around his shoulder blades. I was a bit surprised! In the meantime, she's still waving the crystal around the front of him, and then she moved to his back. As she was waving the crystal up and down, she was not quite reaching the area around his shoulder blades. I thought to myself, "It's higher, higher..." But, she missed that area.

Then she took a big eagle feather and waved and whooshed it over the front of his body and over his entire back. Looking again at his outline image in my mind's eye I saw the black-grey fog start to dissipate as she waved the eagle feather over his upper back.

When she was done she asked the gentleman how that was for him and if he felt better. He said at first when she waved the crystal around him he didn't feel any change in his back pain but it was only after she started waving the feather around him that he said his pain actually went away! I was surprised there seemed to be a correlation to what I saw intuitively, and I realized that my intuition shows me pain in someone's body as a black-grey fog.

Sometime later, when there was a break in the session, I nonchalantly went to have a friendly talk with the gentleman whose back was hurting. I wanted to find out exactly where his pain was, because he never told us. But I wanted to find out surreptitiously. We talked about how that demonstration showed the crystal healing really worked and he said yes he felt a lot better. I asked him where exactly was his pain? He said in his upper back and pointed to it with his thumb. "Around here," he said. I added, "You mean around your shoulder blades?" He responded, "Yes." Ah! That helped me validate that what I was seeing intuitively was correctly pointing out where his pain was using this method.

Now when I do energy healing I use this tool to see the pain and "disease" in people's energy field, which tells me the place in their physical bodies. I have continued to validate my findings by later asking people to verify what is going on in their bodies. My intuition always shows me the pain in a black fog-like mark over the image of their body in my mind. You can do the same as you practice with someone else to find where their pain or "dis-ease" is located.

STEP-BY-STEP

1. Ask your intuition to show you where someone has a physical problem in his or her body.
2. Imagine in your mind a silhouette, or an outline of the person's body you want to energetically scan. A variation would be to imagine that you are, in your mind, scanning someone's body like the light beam that goes down the page on a copy machine. As you scan you can also move the image of the body in your head. Turn it around and get a better view from another angle.
3. Be open and see what intuitive "pop-ups" come in regard to the image in your mind. You are just presenting the canvas of the silhouette or the outline representing the person's body and allowing your intuition to present you with messages.
4. Again, you may see the image in your mind change, or you may hear a word or receive a feeling. These are all the intuitive pop-up pieces that you are being given. For example, you can ask more questions regarding those pieces. "Why are you showing me X?" "Why did you give me the word Y?"
5. If you are doing this as an intuition exercise you can then validate what you received with your partner.

Alternatively you can do this:

1. Ask your intuition to show you where someone has a physical problem in his or her body.
2. Pass your hand over someone about 4 to 6 inches over their body in the air. You don't need to touch them because you are passing your hand through their auric field, which can extend many feet out from a body.
3. As you pass your hand over them slowly, pay attention to what the surface of your hand feels like. You can also pay attention to what your hand is feeling in general. You may feel it tingle, feel cooler or warmer. You may find as you pass your hand slowly it

feels like it is being repelled or maybe feel a little heavier or dip at various places involuntarily. These are all intuitive messages. You may even feel something in your own body but it's not you, it may be an intuitive message simulating what is going on in the person you're scanning.

4. Note what is popping up in your mind. Everything you hear, see or feel in your mind or outside of you is part of the intuitive message being received. Remember your feelings may be emotional as well.

8. Energy Scanning Places

Along with people, you can also scan the energy of a place. All places hold energy that comes from the physical objects in the place. The energy can be from natural objects such as plants, the land, the animals, or from man-made objects, statues, artwork, a car, the buildings, etc. The people who were present or used the space there can also leave behind energy.

Normally, people going through strong emotional events leave the strongest energy behind. Places where repeated activities, such as prayer, happen on a regular basis, makes the energy of those activities stronger. It's almost as if the energy is layered on at that spot over and over again.

HOW

You can pick up this energy in a place by scanning it with your intuition the same way you scan a person's energy field shown above. This can be done with your hand, or with your entire body as you physically walk through a space. You can also scan a place by imagining that you are walking through the space and then be open to what your intuition gives you. Your intuition is triggered by your intention to pick up the energy of a space or place and the act of you imagining it or passing through the space.

STEP-BY-STEP

1. Set your intention to pick up the energy and information contained in the energy of a place.
2. Ask your intuition, "Tell me about this place. What is important about this space?"
3. Using your hand or your entire body you can pass either through the space of a place or location.

4. Be open and aware of picking up what your intuition.

5. Everything you see, feel, hear or think, whether in your mind or outside of you is picking up information about this energy. Pay attention to how you physically feel. The feelings are often very, very subtle. Mostly, you may feel physical sensations. Again, they are very subtle and you may miss them at first. It may feel like a buzz or a hum, or a tingling, or a release, warmth, or coolness. It may feel to you as if the air pressure in the room has changed or that the lighting is a little brighter or dimmer. If you feel something focus your attention on it. This often makes it stronger and more apparent to you.

When I clear houses of negative energies I will walk through each room, circling the room, walking along each wall and see what I pick up. This often will tell me where the strongest negative energies are that I need to focus on clearing out. You can also do this in places that make you feel either very good or perhaps a little uncomfortable. You may be able to pick up why it's making you feel uncomfortable or very good.

9. Intuitive Writing and Drawing

Intuitive writing is writing that comes from intuitive messages received from what people call your Higher Self, your Angels, divine guidance, spirit guides, the Universe or All That Is. Through the process, the writer's hand writes messages but is often unaware consciously of what will be written. When working with the angels by asking them to give us messages through writing I will call this Automatic Angel Writing. It is quite easy to do and accesses information from your intuition that is plain and simple.

HOW

As with all these tools, you trigger your intuition by asking a question or presenting a stimulus for your intuition to act on. For intuitive writing you can ask your intuition a question. Then be open and wait for words to pop-up. You may not get full sentences and that's okay. Intuitive writing seems to have general characteristics.

You'll find the sentences usually begin with the words "you" or "we." In the process of writing, there is often a sense or feeling that someone else is talking to you in your mind, even if it sounds like your own voice. It's readily apparent how the message relates to your immediate concerns or issues. This intuition voice is often to the point and not wordy. The sound of intuitive writing is loving and positive. Intuitive writing may ask you to take immediate action, including changing your thoughts or attitude to be more loving. When you are receiving the messages through intuitive writing, at the time, you think the messages are very obvious and simple, but when you read them later they are quite profound.

STEP-BY-STEP

1. First have something to write on and write with, set it comfortably in front of you so you can write. If you are more comfortable typing on the computer, then do that.

2. Set your intention; ask for your intuition to transmit a message from your angels and guides that you will write down.

3. Relax and breathe. If you do a lot of meditation, then breathe and put your mind in that empty place, but do not meditate, meaning, just try to quiet your mind.

4. Be open and be aware of words that pop-up. The words may come as a whisper. It may seem as your own thoughts, but often the words will start and stop. If you hear two or three words, type or write the two or three words. There may be a pause before the next words, but they will come. Do not force it.

5. Begin to write what you receive. Write the words as they pop-up in your mind. Don't worry if they make sense or not, just write them down as if you were taking dictation. Remember you don't need to be in any special state of mind. Just be open, with passive anticipation that you will receive something. Just write what you hear as you hear it. Sometimes you will receive "thought sentences" where you know what you are going to write in total, like a story you know already or a phrase you frequently use. Write that sentence. The harder you try to think the less flow there will be.

6. Accept what you get. You get what you get and you don't get upset. You may always feel that you are making it up, but you may be surprised what comes out later. When you are in a state of connection, your consciousness is elevated, even though you may not be aware of it. You may think what you're writing is

all just so obvious. Later when you go back to read what you received, you may be surprised that it isn't so obvious.

Often times, you'll find you get one word and then as you wait for the second word a few more will come in a group. Again, don't try to finish the sentence; just let the words "pop" up in your head. You'll find you may not know how the sentence will end. That's all okay, just allow yourself to go with it. Accept what you get, don't try to dissect it or analyze it. You may find the way the sentences are phrased isn't always the way you would speak.

As you practice this, it will get easier and flow much more readily. Later, you may find you will receive messages in your mind this way even when you don't intend to. What may surprise you is later when you go back to read your intuitive writing the words will always seem fresh to you, as if you are reading them again for the first time.

10. Choosing Between Two Equal Things

You can create tools out of everyday things so you don't have to bring your angel cards with you everywhere. That's the wonderful thing about intuition tools, you can use almost anything if you're creative. Here are some methods using Post It Notes, pictures, maps and choosing between two things.

If you have to choose between two things, you can "try" them in your mind and see what your intuition gives you. Say you have to choose between two items on the menu, two places to go for vacation, or perhaps even two job offers. You can imagine you are moving into the future and that you have chosen one of them. Say you have to choose between A or B. Imagine that you have chosen A and you are now in the future after you've made your choice. Ask your intuition, "What is it like for me now that I have chosen A?" Your intuition will respond. Usually, you will start to have intuitive feelings or perhaps symbols will pop-up regarding your choice. You can then choose B and do the same process. You'll often receive very clear intuitive information regarding each, to help make your decision.

Maps are wonderful tools that you can find anywhere, especially on your computer or smart phone. If you are trying to choose a place to go for vacation, or whatever, you can take out a map and look at the two locations and then tune into your intuition by asking it, "Which place is better for me to go to?" It is important to just look at the map as if it were a picture and be open. Don't think about where you should go, but let your intuition answer. The tool can also help you get out of your thinking mind, especially when you're stressed about what choice to make.

I used this technique on a flight from Phoenix back home to New York. I was supposed to fly from Phoenix through Dallas to New York, but there were severe thunderstorms in Dallas at the time. My flight was delayed and they said it could be canceled. I asked the ticket agent if there was another flight to New York I could get on. There was but that flight had a stopover in Los Angeles and was leaving in a few hours. It meant I would get home very late. Suddenly, we were called to board the through Dallas flight! Yay! Got on board the plane and we started to taxi out. While we were waiting on the tarmac to take off, the captain came on and said that he had bad news; we had to turn around and go back to the gate. *BUT*, he said we'd either be delayed or the flight would be canceled, so if the passengers wanted to get off at the gate, we could, but we would not be able to re-board the plane.

Now I didn't know what to do. Should I get off and take the Los Angeles flight, definitely get home but very, very late and perhaps not have my luggage follow me on time? Or, should I risk staying on the through Dallas plane, and possibly have the flight canceled and end up staying in a hotel? I tried tuning into my intuition, but I could tell my emotions started to get in the way. I really wanted to get home fast but my mind was not settled enough to get a good intuitive message.

Then I had an idea; I'll use a tool! I took out the airline magazine they have in the back seat pocket and opened it to the map they always have in the back pages. I asked my intuition, "Which is the best city for me to fly through to get home?" as I gazed over the map. I noticed that the letters spelling out "Dallas" seemed a little darker than the ones for "Los Angeles" and my intuition seemed to be making Dallas stand out. So I decided to stick with going through Dallas. A short time later, we were cleared for takeoff, we flew through Dallas without any further delays and I arrived in New York only a couple of hours late with my luggage!

You can use pictures, write or draw your choices on a Post It Note and allow your intuition to help you choose by these items triggering your intuition as you ask it, "Which one is best for me?" You may find your intuition gives you an indication of which one to choose through something you see, feel or hear in your mind.

CHAPTER 7

How to Make Your Intuition Reliable and Consistent: (B)e Open Is the Secret

• • • • • • • • • • • • • •

To make your intuition reliable and consistently give you accurate information, you need to "get out of the way" so you can receive a clear message. We stop our ability to clearly hear what our intuition is telling us because we cut it off before we hear the entire thing, we mangle its message, we ignore it and we judge it.

Imagine for a moment that you are Your Intuition. You have a simple clear message to give to your Thinking Mind. As Your Intuition, your message is short, and complete, but every time you whisper it to your Thinking Mind, it's not paying attention. It's too busy talking to itself. Then when you finally get its attention, you start to tell Thinking Mind your intuition message, and your Thinking Mind cuts you off and attempts to finish your sentence. As Your Intuition, you don't have many words or resources to use to get your message across; in fact, you only have a short time period before the Thinking Mind attention window closes. Sometimes it seems like you're shouting your message before that window closes but your Thinking Mind is getting distracted and misses it. Other times you're telling your Thinking Mind something brand new, but your Thinking Mind says it's the same old story and distorts what you're trying to say. Coming up with the wrong conclusion or not receiving the message is why the Thinking Mind thinks you, Your Intuition, are unreliable and inconsistent. It's not you… it's your Thinking Mind. This is why your Thinking Mind must quiet itself down, sit still, be relaxed, patient and be open so it can hear what Your Intuition is trying to tell it.

How do you be still, relaxed, patient and open? You'll first have to practice because you're in such a habit of thinking, and thinking a lot. Actually, this is why Esther Hicks, who intuitively channels Abraham, says she is such a good channeler. She is able to turn her thinking mind down and just be. In her words, when she's riding in the car, she'll just gaze out the window and in her mind is, "cow, cow, tree, bush, fence," as she's passing them by. She's relaxed, open and still. Her mind isn't thinking about what she's seeing.

The thinking mind is analyzing, judging, commenting, and often is distracted into thinking and analyzing something else. That's what it does, that's its job. In Esther's case, if her thinking mind was getting in the way, it would go something like this, "Cow, oh a cow, how cool, I wonder what kind of cow that is, why are cows here? I didn't know cows come in that color brown. Gosh, cows are big, how does one get a cow back in the barn? They look kind of cute. I wouldn't want a cow as a pet though." But you have to get control over your thinking mind. You really do. Even if for a moment or two you can stop your mind from analyzing, judging, commenting and getting distracted. One of the ways you get control over your mind is by being open.

What Is It Like to "Be Open"?

What is it like to be open? The best way to understand it is to think of an experience you already know of as being open. As I pointed out in the 10 Key Secrets to Intuition, one of the most important keys is, "Where's the bathroom?" Normally, when you ask this question, you pause and wait for the answer. *That's what being open is.* The state of mind you're in when you've asked your intuition a question should be the same state when you ask the question "Where's the bathroom?" Pause now and remember a time when you were in a new place, you really needed to go to the bathroom and you asked someone where it was. As you paused to hear the answer, you were not thinking, you were just quietly waiting and you were "all ears" listening carefully so you would get it right. Then whatever answer you got you believed. You weren't second-guessing the answer, at least I hope not, and you weren't judging the answer.

Why "Where's the bathroom?" Is Important

Most people don't judge the answer to "Where's the bathroom?" Similarly, you don't judge the answer a waiter gives you when you ask, "What's on the menu today?" You're more likely to act on the information than sit back and judge it. This is exactly the state of mind you have to be in to receive intuitive messages. If you can remember this, it will help you receive clearly your intuitive messages. Later we'll cover how intuitive messages appear to you and what it's like to experience them. But for now, just know being in that open state of mind is important. Don't let Thinking Mind get in the way.

Another important thing to note is that being open and quiet is also *NOT* a state of meditation. You may have heard that when you wait for an intuitive message to appear you have to go into a light trance-like meditative state of mind. This is not necessary. In some techniques, a trance-like state of mind is an open mind and may work for some people to help receive intuitive messages, but it's often difficult for many people to understand how to do that.

Intuition Pop-Ups

Now you know how to be open, what is it you're waiting for? You're waiting for an intuition pop-up. My husband, who is very intuitive, uses the term "pop-up" to describe his intuition. Why call it a "pop-up"? Because that's how intuition seems to appear, it just pops up. Remember, intuition is "Knowing without knowing how you know it." Now we'll add one more point, it pops up. It may be a feeling, part of an image; it may be a word or two that pops up in your mind. But, just know that everything that you see, feel or hear, inside or outside of you is part of your intuition talking to you. Your intuition can even appear as a thought, though you need to be careful to notice whether the thought popped up from your intuition, or whether your Ego is doing some thinking to create that thought. Again, I'll go into more detail in a later chapter on the different characteristics of how intuition comes to you so you can tell the difference.

How Long Does It Take?

A very common question students ask me is, "How long do I have to wait for my intuition to respond to a question?" Once you ask your intuition a question the intuitive response is immediate. You don't need to wait. You are always thinking, feeling, seeing and experiencing something. Just know that your intuition is guiding you to experience these things and they are part of your intuition speaking to you. Often you may miss your intuition's messages because they are short, fleeting and very subtle. You may even say to yourself, "Did I just feel something? Did I just hear something?"

What is the experience of receiving an intuitive message? Intuition messages are short, to the point, non-emotional, and often repetitive. Again, they can be fleeting and subtle. Your intuition will never be disparaging and will never put you down. Messages sound like statements of fact.

For example, you may hear in your mind: "Go left." "Take this one, not that one." You may have a feeling of being repelled or attracted to go in a particular direction. If you are visually looking at choices, one may look clearer, sharper, brighter, prettier or darker than the others.

Even in times of crisis or danger where your intuition is warning you, it will never scream at you, nor will it be hysterical. I experienced an example of this driving home one day.

"Get Behind the Green Car"

One sunny Sunday afternoon I was driving back home from upstate New York. I was driving in the left lane, when in my rear view mirror I saw a large black SUV barreling down behind me. Knowing he wanted to pass me I decided to move out of his way to the right lane, but just ahead of me in that lane was a green car. I thought to myself, "Should I get in front of the green car or behind the green car?" Immediately I heard in my head, "Get behind the green car." As I got closer to the green car, getting ready to over-take it, I thought, "Really? Behind the green car?" Then I heard it again, the same way, calmly and as if it were a matter of fact, "Get behind the green car." I thought, "Okay, I'll get behind it." As I slipped behind the green car in the right lane, the large SUV whooshed past me in the left. Two seconds later we went under an overpass and my husband, sitting in the passenger side, pointed upward to the overpass and said, "Look!" He was pointing to a police car perched atop the bridge with a radar gun to catch speeders. Sure enough, another police car flew down the ramp and onto the parkway, then pulled the SUV over. Had I not listened to my intuition speaking to me, I would have sped up to get in front of the green car and most likely would have been the one to get the speeding ticket instead of the SUV.

That's how your intuition will give you a message. In this case, yes, it was an actual sentence rather than a word or two. But it was short, and to the point. It was calm and not excited. It didn't yell and scream at me with a warning that there was a speed trap ahead and that I might get a speeding ticket. My intuition just said, "Get behind the green car." That was it. It was also repetitive and the message was given in the same way each time. It wasn't expected. It just popped up. Interestingly though, it was responding to a question I was asking myself. But, this time it wasn't my thinking mind that answered, but rather it was my intuition. Also, the important thing is that I listened and acted on the message. That action helped me recognize it was my intuition talking to me.

This message came through to me after several years of practice working with my intuition. As you practice you will become familiar with how your intuition gives you messages and more importantly, what it is like to experience your intuition speaking to you. You might say that you will become familiar with the sound of your intuition's voice in your head. The key right now is to understand that intuitive messages are short, to the point and non-emotional.

In the next chapter we'll go into more detail on how to tell a true intuitive message from when you are making it up, that is, your thinking mind is getting in the way. True intuitive messages have particular characteristics, as we've mentioned.

What If I Don't Get Anything?

A common question that students ask is, "What if I don't get anything?" You will always get something because you are always hearing, feeling, seeing and yes, thinking because thoughts go through your head that are from your intuition. If you get confused or you feel you are too wrapped up in your thinking, then you have to stop and try a different tool or method. We've gone over some tools in the previous chapter. If you're having trouble receiving a response from your intuition tool I recommend you use oracle cards because they are easy to use. Oracle cards help get you out of your "Ego space," and this is why I like oracle cards for beginners.

A Tool to Help You Be Open

Oracle cards are a form of divination tool that people use to get divine guidance. They were historically used to predict the future or receive prophetic messages through using them. Oracle cards are used as a way for your intuition to guide your attention. More importantly, cards can help force you to be open and get you out of your thinking mind or your "Ego space." This is because you don't know which card will pop up when you flip it over to look at it. As a result, because a flipped card can reveal something unexpected, it may force you to focus on what pops up from your intuition rather than try to make up an answer using your thinking mind. I'll give you an example.

One of my first ever experiences doing intuitive readings for the public really pushed me to be open and focus on what was popping up in me intuitively rather than being able to figure out an answer to the intuition question asked.

I was doing a reading for a gentleman; I'll call him Jim because I don't remember his name. Jim was a guy's guy, dressed in jeans and a tight black t-shirt, which revealed that he obviously worked out and had a nice tan. He sat down in front of me and leaned back in his chair with one hand on his hip. I wasn't sure whether the look on his face was a hint of skepticism or just not knowing what to expect. I asked him if he had a specific question in mind or just wanted a general message. He said a general message is fine. Giving a general message to someone is actually difficult for your Thinking Mind to make up something specific, so that forces you to rely more on your intuition and pay attention to your pop-ups. I took my angel cards and shuffled them, drawing out one card at a time. The first one was an angel that looked like cupid with pink colored bubbles in the shape of hearts floating up into the sky. I gulped. The second card was an angel holding a baby, obviously singing a lullaby from the rainbow swirl coming from her with musical notes amongst the colors. I paused and my thinking mind thought, okay, these cards don't look like they fit Jim at all!

Instead of getting scared and succumbing to my Thinking Mind making something up, I stuck to the technique. I allowed myself to be open and just notice what popped up at me, whatever it might be. I knew that my intuition is the conduit through which the angels send messages. My eyes were drawn to the musical notes. I seemed to stare at them involuntarily. I asked my intuition silently, "Why are you showing me these musical notes?" Staying open to receiving an intuitive pop-up what came was, "It's his music." Then at this point my eyes were attracted to the heart bubbles on the other card. I asked my intuition, "What do these hearts have to do with the message?" Again, being open, and waiting for a response I felt intuitively they were connected to the music. I told Jim, "The angels are telling me that you love music." Jim nodded yes.

I asked a few more questions to my intuition, such as "Why are you showing me that he loves music?" The response was, "He creates it." I then asked a few more questions to get more detail and information. My intuition told me that he no longer creates music and he should go back and do more. I relayed this to Jim, "Your angels are saying that not only do you love music but you love to create it. You don't do it anymore and they are say-ing you should create more music." Jim looked surprised, and stammered, "Yes actually, that's amazing." He went on to tell me that he was, what he called, "a closet composer." He actually was a TV producer and writing music wasn't his day job. He explained, that he used to write music at night. He would compose and play his music so late into the night that his wife would complain he was keeping her up. He had stopped composing music for a while now and really missed it. I said, "Well, the angels want you to go back to it." I found out later that his wife was the one who brought him to have an angel reading and that he really didn't believe in "this stuff." But the reading really surprised him and he was now more of a believer.

This is a good example of why it is really important not to edit or judge what you are receiving. It is good to have no expectation of what the mes-sage should or would be! Remember, your intuition is relaying a message you may not have considered. Constantly going back to a "Being Open" state of mind after you ask your intuition a question will help you receive and collect the intuition message pieces. Even though my Thinking Mind was dismissing the cards that were turned over for Jim, I ignored it and was open to whatever my intuition was giving me. In this case I followed what my intuition was drawing me to.

Highlighted Tips and Summary

- *BE OPEN* by remembering what it is like when you ask the ques-tion, "Where's the bathroom?"
- Keep your thinking mind out of the way.
- Remember that your intuition will always answer a question you ask it.
- Your intuition will answer immediately; you don't have to wait.

CHAPTER 8

How to Know You're Not Making It Up: (C)ollect Real Intuition Messages

• • • • • • • • • • • • • •

If you're a highly sensitive person, you may know that your intuition is working for you, but not be too clear on what it is telling you. If you're not a highly sensitive person you may wonder if you even have intuition. Know that you do have intuition; we all have intuition, though you may have not recognized it.

A common problem is feeling your intuition is telling you something important but you don't know if you are just "making it up" or if it's real. Many people ask questions such as, "Sometimes I feel an energy running down my arm, what is that?" or "I keep seeing these faces popping up in my mind, is that my intuition telling me something?" or "I keep hearing this name over and over, is that a message? What should I do with it?" If you're not sure if you have intuition, you may be wondering if any of your thoughts or feelings are intuition or not. This is especially true for those who are just starting to work with their intuition and learning how to get it under their control. It is a common experience for those stuck in Step 2 of the Intuition Learning Path described earlier.

The best way to demystify intuition is by knowing the specific characteristics of a true intuitive message that indicates that it is real. In this way, you can understand the ways intuition can appear to you and how to distinguish it from your thinking mind.

In this chapter we will go over how to know you're not making it up and how to work with your intuition to understand the message.

What Is the Collect Step?

The third step in the technique is to collect your intuition pop-ups. There are two key components of this step. The first is to know whether the intuition pop-up you received is a true intuitive message or not. The second is to remember that the pop-ups you receive are only pieces. You will need to collect the true intuition pop-up pieces so they can reveal the full message. These pieces will form a bigger picture and meaning, which will become apparent to you. It is like walking through a fog in a place that you haven't been to before. All you can see is the path before you and images of objects in your surroundings, as you get closer to them. The more objects you see, the more you are able to know where you are. Then as the fogs clears you can see the entire landscape as it is slowly revealed. It is the same with your intuition as it "speaks" to you. When you know the characteristics of true intuition and how your intuition speaks to you, and collect only those true pieces, they will form the full meaning. You'll then be able to receive and understand your intuition messages clearly.

The next chapter will explain the intuition technique end to end and give you examples of how to use it. For now, it is important to understand how to collect your intuition pop-up pieces first by understanding what real intuition is like and its characteristics. Just to recap, the intuition technique is A+B+C+D+P. A is to ask your intuition a question silently in your mind. B is to be open, and C is to collect your intuition pop-up pieces.

The most important thing to remember about this step is not to be dismayed over what you receive. This is the most important step of the technique. Don't give up on the first cryptic message or pop-up piece you get if you want to get a real intuitive message. Keep in mind, you won't always know what your intuition is going to tell you.

You've asked your intuition a question in your mind silently. You're now open, waiting for your intuition to answer the question with a pop-up piece. You're probably wondering, "How do I know what a real intuition pop-up piece is?" Let's begin explaining that by characterizing intuition. It may be helpful if you think of your intuition as another "being" within you. Let's call her Intuition.

Intuition – How She Speaks to You

Intuition is always with you, always communicating with you. You may not have noticed her. Sometimes she's only revealed when someone says to you, "How did you know that?" Her voice is very subtle, soft and gentle. She is never obtrusive and can be so quiet that it seems like she's speaking to you in a whisper, which you barely notice. She shares her feelings with you easily and you deeply empathize, sometimes thinking they are your own feelings.

You can ask her a question and she will always respond. You'll have to pay close attention because her answer will not come in lengthy sentences and long explanations.

She is always kind and patient. Intuition never reprimands you nor does she yell or shout. She is always calm, collected, steady and to the point.

Intuition is like protective radar. She is always watching over you, and sharing information with you about what is going on around you. She is constantly listening and answering questions you may be thinking, whether you are addressing her or not. Her connection to the Universe, your creator and All That Is allows her to provide you information about all things, whether it is in the past, the present or the future.

The best thing about Intuition is that she is always connected to you, always available and is on your side. She is only focused on your best interest when you need her. Because you are not used to speaking or thinking the way she does, you are not used to her language or her way of communicating. You need to learn how to understand her ways.

Real Intuition Characteristics

Real intuition has several characteristics that help you know it is your intuition that has given you a feeling, a thought, a word or words. These characteristics tend to be quite different from your thinking mind. Real intuition pop-up pieces have these characteristics:

- Non-judgmental
- Non-emotional
- Short and to the point
- Fleeting and subtle
- No "I" in it
- Symbolic

Let's take each one at a time:

Real intuitive messages are **non-judgmental**, meaning they won't criticize you. The messages will not put you down, or build up your Ego. For example, your intuition will never say, "you're stupid," "you should have done better," "you're the greatest," or "you are not good enough." Instead, your intuition may, for example, give you a message that says, "do this instead," "try this action," "don't worry about so and so."

Real intuition is **non-emotional**. Intuition gives you messages as facts or statements but is never screaming at you or excited in tone. As in my last story about the green car, the message was simply, "Get behind the green car." There's a wonderful story about a woman's intuitive experience one foggy night after a big storm. This woman was driving down a dark country road in the fog and came upon a red light that seemed to stay red for a very long time. She couldn't see beyond it too well, and couldn't understand why the light didn't change. Since she didn't want to drive through the light she got out of her car to see if anything was wrong. Just beyond the "light" she saw the storm had washed out the bridge ahead over a raging river that she was headed straight for. Had she continued to drive through the fog she would have driven into the river. Her intuition just made her stop by showing her a red light. There was no excitement, no screaming, or no extreme emotion in the message.

Real intuitive messages or pop-ups are **short and to the point**. The thinking side of our minds likes to come up with logic, rationale, reasoning and long explanations to answer questions. Our intuition is short and to the point when answering a question or giving us a message. This is particularly true when our intuition is speaking to us in words. You may hear your intuition in your mind say, "Go left," "Exit now," "Take that one," "Leave," "Stay close" or simply one word, such as "Stop." Given that intuition will also give you pop-ups that are pieces of the entire message, you may just receive a word that doesn't make sense to answer your question. For example, say you ask your intuition the question, "What does my boyfriend think of me?" and your intuition gives you the word "apple"; just remember it is only a part of the entire message. The one word "apple" is part of a bigger picture and meaning. This is where the collecting begins. You keep the intuition pop-up pieces in mind and can then ask your intuition another question regarding that piece. So the follow up question would be, "Why are you giving me 'apple'?" Your intuition will then respond and give you another pop-up piece.

Remember, this is another way to know whether thinking mind is making up an answer or if you are receiving a real intuitive message. If what you receive is a long-winded and wordy, it, probably, is not your intuition.

Real intuition messages are **fleeting and subtle.** Sometimes you have to replay the intuitive message in your mind, especially if you did not trigger your intuition with a question and you received a pop-up randomly. You might even say to yourself, "Did I really hear something?" or "Did I really feel that?" Here's an example. My husband and I were looking to buy a single family home. We had narrowed it down to two houses. Each of them was pretty much the same as the others in price, size and amenities. Only one was in a gated community with a Home Owners Association's rules and by-laws. I was hesitant to live in a gated community. After visiting that house I remember, as we drove away, I noticed a patch of daisies in the back yard. The flowers were a dazzling brilliant white standing together in this patch. They drew my attention for a moment as being surprisingly unusual and I thought, "Wow, those daisies look like they're shining!" It turned out that we bought the house in the gated community with the daisies. There were no words with the daisies, nothing more than a fleeting and subtle message saying pay attention to this house.

Real intuition will **not use the word "I" in its message**. This is because your Ego is 100% non-intuitive. Your intuition is neutral and not concerned about your pride or placing you on a pedestal. Your intuition will not send you a message that says, "I need to change jobs" or "I am way better than her."

Real intuition will often use **symbols instead of words**. Inside of you, for example, in your mind's eye you may see a color, a picture or even a word that has symbolic meaning rather than being literal. Outside of you, your intuition may direct your attention to a sign that is either literal or symbolic. The symbols can have the same meaning if you experience them inside or outside of you. This is because your intuition uses its own language that is made of symbols having meaning uniquely for you. Your intuition will present to you a symbol over and over again, which will have the same meaning. This is how you can tell what the symbol means. Some symbols will be obvious to you, others not as much. For me, the color gray is a symbol for intense emotions that are either sadness or depression. John Edward, a famous psychic medium, says his symbol for love is a pink rose.

You should write down your symbols as you discover them through doing your intuition exercises, or if you just notice it when your intuition gives you a message. As you write your symbols down you'll build your own lexicon or dictionary of your own symbols that are unique to you. It is better to create your own dictionary of symbols than to buy a book of symbols. Not all symbols in books will have the same meaning for you. Your intuition knows you intimately and will share with you symbols that have meaning that you can relate to.

One student discovered her symbol for serious illness when she was doing an intuition exercise in my class. The students were being shown a photograph of two people smiling on the beach on a sunny day. The intuition exercise was to pick up intuitively as much about the events in the photograph as they could. This particular student's intuition gave her "funeral." She said she didn't know why she received "funeral" and couldn't make sense of it. In working with her, I asked her, "What does funeral mean to you?" She said, "Well, I don't know, I guess they are sad." Pressing further to see if this was more symbolic, I said, "What happens when you go to funerals, what does it feel like?" She then said, "I don't like to attend funerals. Funerals make me feel ill for the next few days."

It turns out that one of the two people in the photograph was actually seriously ill and was hospitalized a couple of days later. The significance of the photograph for the person in the picture was all about this illness. This exercise showed that for this student "funeral" is associated strongly with being ill, which seems to be her symbol for illness.

This is how you may discover your symbols and the symbols that your intuition uses to communicate a message to you. This is also a good reason to exercise your intuition as much as possible. You will become more aware of the symbols and their meanings. That is how I discovered that red is my symbol for anger. When I first started intuitive readings for the public using angel cards, on several occasions, cards that had a red color stood out to me. Red is usually a color that can mean love, passion, high energy or conflict. When the color red pops up using the cards, I would ask my intuition, "Why are you showing me red? What is its meaning?" The answer I most often received was, "Anger." The following illustrates how I discovered this.

I did a reading for a woman who initially wanted me to give her a general message. The cards I drew for her had one card that caught my attention. It was predominantly red. The picture was a stylized gothic drawing of an angel sitting and working at a desk. Below are the questions I asked my intuition and the flow of responses.

I remember this reading in particular because red was a dominant theme of the message. In this example, some of the answers from my intuition were in words, some in feelings, some in abstract pieces of thought, but I will put them in words for clarity. Remember the questions I asked were in my mind addressed to my intuition. I did not speak them out loud.

Me: "Who does this angel represent?"

My intuition: "Your sitter."

Me: "What is this angel doing?"

My intuition: "Working by creating something."

Me: "What is she creating?"

My intuition: My eyes were then drawn to some sort of crown on the angel's head that seemed to be made of beads.

Me: "Why are you showing me this headdress?"

My intuition: "Jewelry."

Me: My attention was drawn to the red color in the drawing. "What does the red color represent, is it love?"

My intuition: "Anger."

Me: "Who is she angry with?"

My intuition: "Someone she works with."

Me: The red color seemed to surround and predominate the picture.

From this, I told the sitter that I was getting that she is working on creating something with her hands, that I was receiving that it was jewelry and that there was anger regarding the work that involved another person. She validated this by telling me she was in a partnership with another woman to create jewelry and that she was having a lot of trouble with her partner on how to conduct the business. She went on to say there was a lot of anger and they were always arguing. You can receive a color as a symbol and it may be a frequent way for you to receive a symbol because we tend to be very visual as humans. Colors have strong associations with meaning and feelings for us. There are many things that can become symbols for you. You will need to determine which symbols have what intuitive meanings for you.

Intuition That Comes from Outside of Us

It may be a surprise to you, as it was to me, that intuition can come from outside of you. Remember, everything that you see, feel or hear is part of your intuitive message, even those things that are outside of you. You may see an actual physical sign, which can also be a literal sign or symbolic. You just might overhear a conversation that just happens to give you the perfect answer you need. You may also be guided to a person, maybe even a stranger, who tells you the perfect thing you need to do next.

This works because everything is connected to the energy of the Universe since everything is part of that energy. You may find you are drawn to a place, a person, a book, a store, right after you asked your intuition for help. That feeling of being attracted or drawn is the answer from your intuition. You may find through synchronicity you are guided by your intuition to the right person, place or thing you needed.

Here's an example of how remembering that intuitive messages can come from the outside, as well as collecting the pieces, helped me read for someone. It was during an intuitive mediumship reading where I was connecting with a sitter's passed loved one. It came about that the person I connected with was her mother who had died a while back. I asked my intuition, which connects to your psychic mediumship abilities, more about her mom. My eye was drawn to a glass of water that was sitting in front of me. Otherwise, I wasn't receiving anything else. I then remembered everything outside is part of the intuitive message as well. I asked my intuition, "Why are you showing me this glass of water?" The intuitive answer was, "Fear." I asked again, "What does fear have to do with the glass of water?" I received, "Water," and a feeling that the fear was very intense and that it was related to drowning. I told my sitter that I was getting her mother had a fear of water, that she had an intense fear of drowning. She said, "Yes, that's right, my mother had a huge fear of drowning. She hated the water she was so afraid. She never wanted any of us to go swimming because of it."

This shows not only do we receive intuitive information outside of us, because our intuition draws our attention to certain external objects, but also how you collect the pieces of information your intuition presents you which then forms the message.

Why Experiencing Your Intuition Is Important

Without knowing exactly how intuition comes uniquely to you, you'll never be able to recognize it. The only way to know how intuition comes to you is to experience it for yourself. The power in knowing what it feels like, sounds like and is like for you, will definitively and positively identify a real intuitive message for you the next time you get one.

This is the same with a physical activity like swimming. Reading all the books in the world about swimming, how to swim, what it feels like to someone else, and their describing experiences of swimming does not replace actually swimming yourself to know what it is truly like. You won't be able to swim just from reading books either! You have to do it. This is especially true for intuition because the experience of intuition is a very subtle one. It is subtle in intensity and sometimes the words you hear from your intuition sound like you! You will need to experience your true intuition over and over again to know confidently what your true intuition is like. You can only gain experience by practicing. That is because your once in a while intuitive hits do not give you enough experience to know what true intuition feels like. The good news is practicing does!

Be used to not understanding the message with the first piece. Get used to practice using your intuition on small decisions you make every day, such as: Which sandwich should I pick for lunch? Which parking lot aisle has an empty spot, or the most empty spots? Which way should I go to work that has the least traffic? Remember that your practice should include ways to validate your choice. Did you pick a sandwich that tasted really good and just hit the spot? Did you find an empty parking spot where you think your intuition led you? Did you take the route to work with the least traffic? Many people think that intuition is only good for big important life decisions and that is what they try to practice their intuition on. That is the worst thing to practice your intuition on! You have to practice crawling before you walk, or walking before you run.

Intuition exercises are critical for improving your intuition skills and knowing what a real and true intuition message is. You need to know what it is like when you correctly identified your intuition's pop-ups and pieces. This helps prepare you to use your intuition on tough life decisions.

Highlighted Tips and Summary

- Collect your true intuition pop-up pieces by recognizing them as real intuitive messages first.
- Your intuition speaks to you in her own quiet language of symbols, pictures, words and feelings.
- Knowing the characteristics of a real intuitive message will help you recognize them.
- Intuition can give you messages by using your external world.
- Experiencing your own intuition will give you the ability to always know when you're not making it up.
- You must practice using your intuition to get yourself ready to use it on tough life decisions.

CHAPTER 9

Breaking Intuition Down

. . . .

The Different Ways You Can Receive Intuition

We sense and pick up information about our world through our senses of seeing, hearing, feeling, tasting and smelling. This is also how we receive our intuitive messages; through images, sound, feelings, etc. How we sense these messages is usually in our minds though sometimes we can actually sense intuitive messages physically outside of us. There are metaphysical theories that explain how these metaphysical senses actually work.

Many intuition and psychic development books talk about the "clairs." The first use of "clair" came from the word "clairvoyant" which in French means "clear seeing." The word clairvoyant was extended to mean having psychic gifts or seeing the future. Clairvoyance was originally known to be the visual psychic sense. Clairvoyance then morphed to describe other psychic senses: for hearing "clairaudience," for feeling "clairsentience," for thoughts "claircognizance" and taste and smell being "clairgustance" and "clairalience" respectively.

People often claim that they are clairvoyant, clairaudient or clairsentient to describe their type of psychic ability. This gives others the impression that a particular psychic sense is bestowed upon you as a gift and therefore you are that gift. But, you are not just a seeing person, so why should you be only clairvoyant? I believe you can develop all your intuitive senses! Remember you are a seeing, feeling, hearing person. You also taste, smell and have feelings. If you are not clairvoyant you can be. If you are not clairsentient you can be.

When you use more of your physical senses you receive more intuitive and psychic information to build the intuition message story. Everyone has all the senses and therefore can have all the intuitive senses. You just need to develop your intuitive senses by practice and knowing how you receive your intuitive messages through them. Let's go over each sense and the ways you can receive intuitive pop-up pieces.

Images That Are Intuition

One way we receive our intuitive messages is through images or parts of images of things we see inside our minds or outside of ourselves. These images can be just a color, a fragment of an image, or a more detailed picture. Both seeing in your mind's eye or outside of you is a way you can receive intuitive messages through images.

Seeing in the "mind's eye" is commonly misunderstood. In working with students, I was surprised to find there is confusion over what "seeing in your mind's eye" means to them. Many people don't know what it's like to have pictures in their mind or have "mind's eye" misconceptions. Let's go over these misconceptions and myths, which may help you understand how real intuitive images can be received.

MYTH 1   *"Clairvoyant images are seen outside the body and are in full in-depth color and high-definition detail."*

Most people who receive intuitive messages clairvoyantly "see" them in their mind's eye. This includes all the famous psychics and intuitives that you admire. Where are they seeing these images? It is the same place where your imagination creates images. Remember, these are not images outside of you. There also seems to be a misconception of where your mind's eye actually is. It actually isn't any particular place in your head, and even if it is somewhere in your brain, you can't really tell anyway. Some people have been told that if you close your eyes and look at where your third eye is inside your head, that this is where your intuitive images reveal themselves. You don't have to do that, plus I think that may be a bit uncomfortable to do.

Some people actually do see intuitive visions outside of themselves. These people who always see visions outside themselves are rare. Seeing an intuitive image outside may be a rare occurrence for people in general. What people often see outside themselves might be spirits of those people who have passed, or metaphysical energy. The human aura is the metaphysical part of a person that is pure energy. It is this energy that makes up their visions of what is known as auras, or a person's metaphysical energy that extends beyond their body.

Another misconception is that intuitive images are highly detailed and elaborate. The images that you see clairvoyantly are usually not in full detail and they may not be complete. For example, you may intuitively see a face, but only see hair shape and style, while the face features are not clear. Intuitive images are often piecemeal. Many times what you remember of an intuitive pop-up is only a part of the image, but if you try to remember more of the image, you'll realize there was more in the image you saw. For example, you intuitively see a car at first, and then if you go back in your memory to replay the image, you may notice the color, shape or the kind of car in the image.

MYTH 2 *"Experiencing making an image in our imagination is different from a clairvoyant image."*

People expect that an intuitive image is going to be strikingly different from what we experience when we are imagining something. An intuitive image is very similar to an image that you create in your imagination. While we are not making up an intuitive image in our mind, the way an intuitive image comes to us is very similar to what we "see" when we are making up an image in our imagination. The images in your mind's eye may not be as detailed as the ones you see physically. You can try imagining an image for yourself.

Try to recall what your home looks like from the outside, or visualize in your mind the spelling of your name. If you can spell the word "CAT" or your name in your mind by picturing the letters, you can receive intuitive images. This is how the images appear in your mind's eye.

MYTH 3 *"Clairvoyance is something you are born with and cannot be developed, either you have it or you don't."*

Most of us can see, feel, hear, smell and taste. We don't classify ourselves as just a "seeing" person or a "hearing" person, therefore, wouldn't it be logical that we can have all the psychic senses? People feel that they are only clairsentient because they recognize more of their intuitive messages through feeling. But this doesn't mean that they don't get intuitive messages clairvoyantly, or cannot develop clairvoyance. In the beginning of developing my own intuitive skills, I did not receive intuitive messages as images, and always thought being clairvoyant would be awesome. Through practicing intuition development techniques I am now very clairvoyant.

How to Develop Your Clairvoyance

You can develop clairvoyance fairly easily. First, believe that you can develop your clairvoyance, because you are a seeing person. Then, by practicing noticing images in your mind and even creating them through your imagination, you will become more familiar with your "mind's eye." You can further your practice by looking at pictures, photographs, paintings and drawings in magazines, museums and books. You can also look at videos, movies, or just go out in nature or people watch. When you are looking at a picture with your physical eyes, close your eyes and in your mind, imagine the picture you just saw. This will help you become familiar with what "seeing in your mind's eye" means to you.

You can create visually. You can do the old fashion way of creating visually by drawing, painting, and coloring in adult coloring books; create a scrapbook or take photographs. You can also use your computer or tablet to make all kinds of visual creations. There are applications to draw, "paint," or make collages with digital photos. The opportunities are endless. You may even find creating a video for YouTube is something you like using your sense of vision for.

There's nothing mysterious about how to receive clairvoyant intuitive messages. It's important to remember the images are not detailed and may be just pieces of an image. Practice your clairvoyance and you may soon find that you're receiving intuitive messages through those pictures in your mind.

The Difference Between False and
True Intuitive Message Images

Real intuitive messages that you receive as images have similar characteristics and those images that are false or not real intuitive messages also have their own characteristics. Here are the differences.

These are the characteristics of images that are not real or are false intuitive messages:

- You can easily manipulate the false image in your mind.
- You may feel you are forcing yourself to create the false image.
- The message implied in the false image is Ego-filled, perhaps self-inflating or self-deprecating.

These are the characteristics of images that can be true intuitive messages:

- You see a fragment of an image – remember you may not see an entire picture.
- You may just see a color, or a flash or sparkles.
- The lighting in the room may seem brighter or darker to you.
- You may receive just a flash of an image that can pop up in your mind.
- You see a little movie in your mind that you cannot manipulate.
- Seeing things in your peripheral vision or the corner of your eye.
- You may have vivid and lucid dreams that you can't forget and seem so real.

People who are naturally clairvoyant are visually oriented such as artists, photographers, graphic designers, interior decorators, or just people who like visual things. But remember, if you don't "see" things it doesn't mean you aren't, or can't, be clairvoyant.

Sounds That Are Intuition

You can hear your intuitive messages. Just like receiving an intuitive message through images, you will mostly receive intuitive messages in your mind. This is usually known as your inner voice or that small still voice inside your head. Again, just as receiving images in pieces and portions of an image, you may hear a word or two from your intuition. You may not hear an intuitive message as complete sentences. The intuitive words may not make immediate sense to you, and this is okay. You need a collection of these intuitive pop-up words, which come together to make sense as they form the message. Receiving intuition through words you can hear in your mind or outside of you is called clairaudience.

Clairaudience or "clear hearing" involves hearing your intuitive messages from outside of you or from inside your mind which may or may not sound like your own voice. Sometimes it's hard to tell the difference between your intuition's inner voice and your own thoughts. Real intuitive messages through hearing have common characteristics. Intuitive message words are usually direct, to the point, give distinct instructions, and they are not wordy. For example, you may hear, "Go left now," "Go talk to that person," "Stop" or perhaps, "Pick that one." The good thing about triggering your intuition with a question is that just the act of asking a question often automatically makes you listen.

In the beginning, when you are working with your intuition you'll hear a word or two because it's easier for you to recognize. As you develop your intuition skills you may hear more complete sentences later. Initially you may hear short phrases or pieces of sentences. For example, you hear your name being called or hear music in your head.

You can also hear things that are outside of you. An auditory intuitive message may be something you hear outside of you that catches your attention because it has particular relevance for you. An example would be someone saying just the right thing to you directly or you overhear them talking to another person. Music playing may have lyrics in a song that just happens to play at the time you need to hear it. Out of nowhere, you may detect a whisper of beautiful sounding music that soothes you or puts you in the right frame of mind. You could hear a song repeatedly, over and over again, either in your head or on the radio that has a meaning trying to get through. Have you ever just "happened" to turn on the television or radio at the precise moment when you hear a relevant discussion that has the answers for you? That is your intuition responding to you.

Hearing false messages that you're making it up also have similar characteristics. Remember that the Ego is 100% non-intuitive. The sentences that start with "I" are from your thinking mind and Ego self rather than your intuition. If what you hear is confusing, cryptic or unclear, it is probably your thinking mind and not your intuition. False messages strongly feel like you're talking to yourself. If what you hear is very wordy and vague it is a false message. If what you hear is nasty, puts you down, alarming or cruel to yourself or others, it is a false message. Anything you hear that is gossip or talks about others is not real intuition. Finally, if you hear a message to hurt yourself or others that is a false message.

People who tend to naturally be clairaudient are often musicians, people who love to listen to music, counselors or therapists, and those who use their sense of hearing often for work or play.

Here are some ways to exercise your intuitive sense that comes through hearing. Intuitive writing is a great way to developing your clairaudience since you are practicing receiving words and "hearing" the message that pops up in your mind. Music is a great way to stimulate your sense of hearing, and train you to hear subtle sounds. Spending some time to listen to subtle sounds of nature at night, the sounds of the animals or even the breeze helps hone your listening skills. Listening to classical music is wonderful for learning how to listen to your intuition, particularly complex music such as classical or jazz because it gives you intricacy in listening.

Feelings That Are Intuition

We often experience our intuition most easily as a feeling. It may be a "gut feeling" that something isn't right, or you feel uneasy and can't explain why. This is called clairsentience or "clear feeling" and involves receiving intuitive messages as an emotion or a physical sensation. The feelings are often subtle and are not extreme. These messages can manifest as: a feeling that something is not right in the room, something feels out of place, but everything looks fine. You feel a little tense, but you can't figure out why. The feeling could be pleasing where you suddenly feel peaceful or relaxed and safe. If you've ever felt a change in feelings where seemingly out of nowhere, you suddenly feel sick to your stomach even though before you felt fine and healthy.

Here's a good list of examples of what intuitive feelings can be like and what they possibly can mean:

- You feel butterflies in your stomach, or a feeling of nervousness, again you can't place why. Possible meaning: There is something negative around or near you.
- You feel an urge to go in a different direction or do something different than your normal routine. Possible meaning: Take a different route today physically (such as a different way to work) or symbolically you need to change your path.
- You feel lighter, happier and freer. Possible meaning: You are on the right path, things are going to be better or a resolution is imminent.
- You have a feeling of excitement and a subtle urge to move forward. Possible meaning: Yes! You are going in the right direction, keep going or doing what you're doing.
- Feelings of peace with a knowing that everything is going to be okay. Possible meaning: Your angels are with you and helping you. Your problem is being resolved.

- Feeling a change in the air pressure, it feels like the air is heavier, or lighter. Possible meaning: Angels or perhaps the presence of a passed loved one is near.
- You physically feel a buzz or wave of something like energy run through you. Possible meanings: Pay attention here, there is something you need to notice.
- As you walk through a room or a place, your subtle physical and emotional feelings change as you move from spot to spot. Possible meanings: Depending on the feelings, it may be energy left over from people who have been in the space. Everyone feels energy differently and the meaning of the feeling can be unique to each person. The feeling can mean that you're picking up a nearby person who is either ill mentally or physically. The feeling can be a person nearby who is blessed, gifted and can transmit positive healing energy to others.
- Getting the "chills" that make your hair stand up. Possible meaning: Pay attention here, there is something you need to take notice of, which can be positive or negative.

The feelings are very subtle and you have to pay attention to know that they are there. There are a few ways you can determine if the feeling is a true intuitive message. If you are genuinely receiving intuitive messages through feelings from a particular place or person, you can try to move away and see if the feeling goes away. Then see if they return again when you get close to the place or person. This is the best way I can tell if I am intuitively picking up intuitive information from a place or person.

Here are some examples of false clairsentient feelings:

- You can link the feelings to recent thoughts of worry.
- The feeling is about doubting yourself.
- The feeling that urges you to make big life changes comes with a feeling of desperation, not from a place of peace.
- The feeling is forced, as if you're trying to make guidance happen.
- You can attribute the feeling to something, such as an illness.

People who are naturally sensitive tend to be very clairsentient. Those who have a sensitive stomach are very often quite clairsentient. This was my experience as a young girl. I always had stomach trouble, which often had me running to the bathroom. I was very careful of what I ate for many years, but it didn't always work. When I began to realize that it could be intuitive feelings I was picking up from metaphysical energy, I made sure that I would "test" the feeling first by moving away from what seemed to be the source. Another way to tell that the feelings may not be your own is if the feelings are very strange or unusual for you. In preparing for a retreat I was leading with a colleague, we were picking up one of the attendees at the airport. While she was waiting at the baggage claim to pick up her luggage, I stood near her. Although I was calm before, I suddenly felt like I had to run out of the airport. The feelings were of panic and anxiety, which was strong enough that I had to move away and go sit down. It was very odd; I couldn't explain it because I never have had feelings of panic before. As I sat further away from our attendee, I began to feel better and I realized maybe the feelings were not mine. I found out later that she was being medically treated at the time for panic attacks and anxiety.

Everyone can be clairsentient and pick up intuitive information through feelings whether they are feelings of emotion or physical sensations. You can do an exercise right now to increase your awareness of your intuitive feelings. Practice by being aware of how you're feeling. Ask yourself these questions after you close your eyes. How do you feel right now? Be present and feel your body. Feel what your limbs and body feel like. Do you feel tense anywhere? Do you feel pain or discomfort? If you're sitting, feel the chair against your legs, or if you're writing, feel your pen in your hand. Feel how your joints feel, your feet, your hands or fingers. This will all help you become more aware of your physical body and the intuitive feelings that are transmitted through it.

Thoughts That Are Intuition

You can also receive intuition through a thought. This is not thinking out an answer, and it is not logically deducing a result. Our intuition will pop up a thought that is usually short in number of words or is a complete concept. If your intuition speaks to you in words combined with a thought, it will be brief and complete. It may feel similar to hearing an intuitive message in your mind. Receiving intuition through thoughts is called claircognizance. Claircognizance or "clear knowing" is suddenly knowing something for a fact, without knowing how you know it. Claircognizance sometimes is harder to distinguish from our own thoughts but true intuition thoughts will have a consistency in the way they come to you. Both clairaudient and intuitive messages, as a thought, will have the following similar characteristics of true intuition.

Real intuitive thought message characteristics:

- The intuitive thought is short, specific and distinct.
- If the intuitive thought is a positive one, it often makes you feel energized.
- True intuitive thoughts breed more exciting ideas that naturally feel good.
- The intuitive thought may come out of the blue or in response to prayer.
- The intuitive thought feels true and makes sense.
- The intuitive thought is consistent and repetitive.
- The intuitive thought solves a problem, like an epiphany, in a clear and complete way.
- The intuitive thought provides a definitive next action step to take.
- The intuitive thought is consistent with your natural interests, passions or talents.

Non-intuitive thoughts that you are making it up:

- The thoughts are random and changing all the time.
- The thoughts are about how to get rich quick.
- The thoughts are disparaging, discouraging and abusive.
- Thoughts involve worst-case scenarios and have depressing or frightening thoughts.
- The thoughts revolved around doubt, worry or anxiety.
- The thoughts are vague and confusing.
- Underneath you feel the thoughts are from trying to get the answer you want.

You can improve your ability to receive intuitive thoughts by clearing your mind of judgments. We often develop a habit of criticizing and second-guessing the thoughts that go through our minds. When you do that, you may dismiss the true valid intuitive thought message that you need to hear. You can improve your awareness of your intuitive thoughts by allowing the free flowing thoughts in your mind to come up but then let them go by. Meditation is a perfect practice for this since becoming aware of your thoughts then letting them go is part of meditating.

People who tend to receive intuitive thoughts more easily are generally teachers, writers, engineers, scientists, researchers, etc.

Other Senses of Intuition

You can receive intuitive messages through ways that parallel our other senses such as smell or taste. Clairgustance is "clear tasting" and clairalience is "clear smelling." Picking up intuitive messages through taste or smell is not common but does happen. For example, an intuitive smell may come from out of nowhere, such as jasmine blossoms indicating a coming celebration. These intuitive smell or taste messages can also be symbolic or has meaning for you.

My grandfather was a very strong presence in my life and was very fond of me. He passed when he was 101 years old so I had many years to listen to his stories and spend time with him. When I was a child he came to live with my family for the summer months after my grandmother died. I always remember visiting Grandpa and him smelling minty from the Chinese medicated plasters he used to ease his muscle and joint pain. Years after he died, I believe he came to visit me in spirit. I had just learned I was pregnant with my first child and had just gotten out of bed. I suddenly smelled that distinct minty plaster very strongly in the bedroom, even though we didn't have any in the house! That surely was Grandpa saying how happy he was that he was going to be a great-grandfather, even in spirit!

CHAPTER 10

How to Get Useful, Understandable Information from Your Intuition: (D)o It Again

• • • • • • • • • • • • •

The goal of using your intuition is to get useful, understandable information that has enough detail so you can act on it. The biggest issue you may have with your intuition is feeling that your intuition is telling you something but you don't know what it means or what it is about. This step in the technique shows you how to get detailed, useful information by gathering more pieces from your intuition by asking another question and starting the cycle again to collect enough intuitive pop-ups so you can understand what your intuition is telling you. Keep in mind these message pop-ups are often piecemeal and fragments, therefore gathering them eventually forms the clear picture of what the intuitive message is. With enough real intuition pieces collected, it usually becomes immediately apparent what the overall message means. We'll see how and why this happens.

Putting It All Together with the Cycle of Q&A

Now that you've learned how to get and recognize your real intuition pop-up piece, what do you do with it? If you're just starting out on the Intuition Learning Path you are now paying more attention to your intuition but what you received doesn't make much sense to you. You might feel that your intuition isn't working at all because nothing you initially receive makes sense. You think you've failed. But you didn't. Keep in mind that intuition speaks in a language of pieces, symbols and big picture ideas that we are not used to. Intuition functions in a whole abstract concept way, and we are used to thinking in a sequential, step-by-step way. Our language is serial. This means our language, and pretty much how we think, is comprised of one word after another to create sentences, and then we put sentences, one after the other, together. For us to understand intuition messages, we would rather be told sequentially, sentence by sentence, so it builds an understanding. Your intuition doesn't understand how to communicate step by step. Intuition communicates in all at once ideas. So how do we bridge the gap? By allowing the pieces to come together to form the whole message. Here's an analogy that works well.

If you've ever watched someone paint or draw a picture, you'll see that they do not start from one corner of the page and then go across the page from left to right, then shift down a row and draw more on the next line. That's the way we type words and sentences in our computer or the old-fashioned typewriter. What artists do is they will look at their paper or their canvas and start drawing a bit here in one spot, then in another spot, and then in another spot that seems to be random. Watching them you have no idea what they are drawing or painting unless they told you beforehand. Eventually, as more spots are filled in, the picture begins to emerge and you can recognize what it is.

This is how your intuition gives you information, piece by piece slowly filling in the entire "picture" until it makes sense to you. If I could provide the information in this book in a big picture, holistic way, it would be so much faster than writing. It would be like a complete download into your brain of all the information instantly. But, that would be overwhelming since we don't think or learn that way. You need to bridge between your inability to understand the intuitive presentation of the entire abstract concept and your communication style of receiving information sequentially. This step of doing the cycle again is how we build that bridge.

(D)oing the Cycle Again –
Collecting Useful Intuitive Information

The way you gather the pieces of intuitive messages is by doing the cycle of "Ask, Be Open, Collect" again. By asking your intuition more questions your intuition will respond with more pop-up pieces. This was a revelation for me when studying how to do intuitive readings. You may think that all intuition is just downloads of detailed stories and information because this is what you've witnessed with an experienced intuitive or psychic reader. What they are not showing you is the protocol and process they went through to get that detailed information. They are also just getting bits and pieces of intuitive information initially, but what you don't see is they will constantly go back and ask their intuition for clarification. They are using the intuition technique of Ask, Be Open, Collect, Do It Again. Each intuitive pop-up piece leads to you asking your intuition another question about that piece.

Your first intuitive pop-up will probably be something that doesn't make sense to you, so your next question is to ask for clarity, for example you can ask your intuition, "Can you make this clearer, I don't understand." You can ask your intuition how the pop-up pieces relate to each other. If a piece is particularly odd or unusual you can ask your intuition, "Why are you showing me this?"

Here is an example of how to use the A+B+C+D cycle of asking your intuition questions to get a true clear message. I often use angel oracle cards as a way to get out of my Ego mind and connect to my intuitive side. In using the cards, you don't know what card will come up next so you have to be open to your intuition to get the messages your intuition is telling you. I like to use cards that have detailed and elaborate pictures on them because my intuition often guides my eyes to notice things in the image. Your intuition will often guide you to notice things around you to respond to your questions.

When Jane came to me with her daughter, Linda, to get an intuitive angel reading, this cycle of question and answer came in handy to reveal information that I couldn't have known. They eagerly sat down as I gave them my introduction about angel readings. Jane was very interested in getting angel messages for her daughter, who I was meeting for the first time. Jane didn't want me to be swayed by any outside information, and deliberately told me nothing about her. As I shuffled the cards, I explained that angel readings will give you guidance in life and that their messages come to me through intuition and inner guidance.

Since I didn't know anything about Linda, I asked my angels to tell me what I needed to know about her. This is a good type of question to ask when you don't know what to ask about. By the way, you can ask this question for any situation you want to receive guidance on, "What do I need to know about this situation for my (or so and so's) highest good?"

In asking about Linda, I then flipped over one of the cards in the deck to look at it. The picture had mostly green vegetation on it, as if it were in the woods. But, my eye was drawn to a tiny small stone bench in the picture that had two stone slabs as legs and a stone top. It was so small that you could hardly see it in the drawing. But, I couldn't take my eyes off it. So I asked my intuition another question, "Why are you showing me this stone bench?" The response I intuitively received was "It's not a bench, it's a desk." I followed up with another question, "What does the desk represent?" Another answer came and it said, "Knowledge and the mind." My eye then was drawn to the green around the bench, and I knew by this time my symbol for healing was the color green. I asked another question, "What does the green color and the bench mean?" I then just repeated what I received to Jane and Linda, "They are telling me that your daughter is going to be a healer, but she's not going heal people's bodies, she's going to heal their minds." They both looked surprised and then Jane said, "Yes! Actually, she's now in school studying to be a Clinical Psychologist."

There are two reasons why I like telling this story to students. First, it shows how divination tools, in this case angel cards, can help you really get out of your second-guessing mind and have you rely on getting information from your intuition. The second is demonstrating how the cycle of going through steps Ask, Be Open, Collect and Do It Again really helps gather the intuition pop-up pieces so you can see what the entire message is. You can try this for yourself and you may be surprised at what your intuition receives.

Why Doing the Cycle Again Is Important

It is very important to allow your intuition to form the message for you and not allow your judging mind to deduce or figure out the answer.

Sometimes the message is completely unexpected and you may think what you received is crazy, or so outrageous that it can't be true. You will have a tendency to dismiss it immediately. Don't do this. You may find the most amazing "hits" from your intuition come from the very items you initially thought were crazy. You may want to note down your intuition pop-ups either in a journal or, nowadays, on your smart phone or some device where you can keep track of them. At first the pieces will seem disparate, but as you collect more, their relationship to each other will begin to make sense.

The more you practice using your intuition and improving your hit rate, you will find the cycle of asking questions and collecting the intuitive pop-ups will be second nature. You'll automatically be asking your intuition a series of questions so quickly that the message will form in front of you like someone drawing a picture. It will seem to others that you are getting downloads of detailed information from your intuition. If you are just using your intuition for yourself, you'll find that you can gain intuitive information about any situation, problem or question exponentially faster than using deduction or logic. You'll just know amazing things without knowing how you know it.

How to Do the Cycle Again the Right Way

It is important that each time you ask your intuition a question you are following the process of Ask, Be Open, and Collect. The initial question you ask your intuition will probably be the easiest one because at the start you can be open more easily. Once you've gotten your first few intuitive pop-up answers you may be tempted to make sense of it. We all have a great desire to be right and that pushes us to try to understand how the intuitive pop-up fits into a logical answer. Resist being tempted to think through and possibly forcing the pop-up pieces to fit together.

This also means you need to resist asking your intuition leading questions to try to get the answer you may be looking for. This is like second-guessing that the bathroom is down in the basement, when there is no bathroom in the basement, and then asking someone, "Can you tell me where the bathroom in the basement is?" Then they respond by saying, "The bathroom is down that hallway, the second door on the left." That answer may leave you a bit confused because you were guessing the bathroom is in the basement and asked a leading question that was wrong.

The same thing goes for asking subsequent questions of your intuition after you've received your initial intuition pop-ups. It is important that you ask questions regarding the pop-ups you've gotten so far. Again asking only non-leading questions based on the intuitive pieces you've gotten so far, not on what answer you want or expect to get. It is key to use your thinking mind to pose a question, but not try to come up with or reason out the possible answer. The correct intuitive message will form an answer from the pop-ups as you gather them, it will make sense when you have received enough pop-ups.

An example of a bad "leading" intuition relationship question would be, "How do I stop my spouse from being wrong all the time?" A good intuition question would be, "What could I do to improve my relationship with my spouse?" A bad leading intuition question would be, "How do I make more money now?" A better intuition question would be, "What should I do to increase my business or improve my performance at work?" When you don't know what to ask you can always get a general message by asking, "What general message do you have for me today?"

What Not to Do When Working with Your Intuition

A dangerous path to be on when you are developing your intuition is trying to make everything you think you are receiving from your intuition is a "hit" or a correct answer. Some students just learning to work with their intuition will attempt to morph or twist what they receive into a relevant meaning. This is especially important when you are practicing your intuition with a partner. You don't want to take one intuitive pop-up and then use conjecture to try to come up with a meaning.

Here is an example of where one can have their thinking mind get in the way with their first piece of intuitive information during a practice intuitive reading with someone else. *"I got the word divorce. I feel nervous. Did you have a divorce during this time? Maybe it is about something coming to an end. It could be going separate ways, moving on, starting over. Is it being nervous about something coming to an end?"* You have to collect enough intuition pieces to see what the message means. The intuitive pop-up pieces should then all fit together naturally. Trying to deduce the answers or figuring out what the intuitive message piece is will send you down the wrong path.

Repetition and Practice Makes This Step Automatic

It is vitally important that you practice working with your intuition properly to build your skill. Many times the inclination is to learn the intuition technique and then practice on important life questions such as, "How do I make more money?" "Should I move to another State?" "When should I take that degree program?" This is like having just learned how to drive a car and then going out on the racetrack to compete in a car race. You will need to practice using your intuition frequently. The good news is you can practice easily in the daily things you do where you're using your intuition on non-important decisions or situations.

Here is an example. Suppose you are going to meet your friend for lunch. You can ask your intuition a few things about her or him before you see them. Some questions you would ask your intuition would be, "What is my friend wearing today?" or "What mood is my friend going to be in?" Later in this book there are more intuition exercises you can do to practice.

The best way to practice is to get into a development group where you can practice with a partner. A development group is where people get together to practice their intuition with each other. A common way to practice is to pair up and do intuitive readings for each other. One person will be the "reader" and one person the "sitter." You can also practice with a friend. You may think you know everything about them, but you don't and can still pick up good intuitive information that they can validate for you.

The more you practice the greater your skill will be in determining when it's your intuition giving you information and when your thinking mind is getting in the way. You'll begin to hear your intuition when you aren't expecting it. You'll gain confidence in using your intuition because you'll know for sure what your intuition feels, sounds, or looks like. You'll recognize your intuition immediately. As you use the cycle of asking your intuition a question, and gathering the intuition pop-up pieces that come over and over to form the complete message eventually the cycle will get faster. You'll be able to get detailed information from your intuition more quickly.

When you have honed your ability to use your intuition at your command, you will have more confidence in your decisions by checking in with your intuition when you make them. You no longer will be afraid of making the wrong decision. You'll be more connected to your higher self and your soul. You'll know which is the right path. Your intuition will be there to tell you what to avoid, when to move forward and help you find effective solutions to problems. You won't need others to guide you because you will have guidance from within.

Highlighted Tips and Summary

- Useful understandable information from your intuition comes from the gathering of the intuition message pieces.
- Full meaning of the intuitive message forms like a picture being drawn by an artist.
- Do the cycle of Q&A to gather enough intuition pop-ups to form the complete message.
- Practice your intuition exercises to make your intuition automatic.

PART THREE

Making Your Intuition Useful

CHAPTER 11

How to Get More In-Depth Detail: (P)racticing Intuition Exercises

• • • • • • • • • • • • • •

When it comes to intuition, the phrase, "intuition exercises" is one of the most frequently searched terms on the Internet. This is because intuition exercises not only reveal how well your intuition works but it also gives you a way to improve your ability to make your intuition more tangible. In this chapter I'll explain why you should exercise your intuition, what makes a good intuition exercise and the best way to do an intuition exercise either alone or with someone else. This largely comes from my working with many people to teach them intuition development and seeing what works best to give students the quickest success with their intuition.

Then we'll go over specific exercises you can do alone as well as with a partner. These exercises also serve as examples of what a good intuition exercise is and how you can create infinite variations of these exercises on your own. If you would like to do some intense practice with others you can join an intuition development group, which are also called development circles. We'll go over what they are, how they are run, what makes a good circle or group, how to assess one and how to find one locally.

What Makes a Good Intuition Exercise?

There are good intuition exercises and bad intuition exercises. Like any exercise that is going to directly improve what you are practicing, you need to know how to perform the exercise in a very clear and understandable way. The exercise should contain a technique or method that has steps for you to follow. You also need to be able to measure your results. In this case, you're exercising your intuition, so you'll have to be able to know whether your results are good or not. That means you need to know if you accurately receive an intuitive message that was correct or not. The key here is to be able to validate your results. If you can't validate your results you'll never know if your practicing is effective. It's like learning how to play tennis in the dark. If you can't see where the ball is going after you hit it, you'll never know if it went into the court or not.

Intuition exercises that meet all the criteria are often hard to find. You can find many so called "exercises for your intuition" but these are really just things to create a life style, not true intuition exercises. What are intuition exercises that are not truly exercising your intuition? Here are some examples found on the web: clear your mind, imagine, journal, dream, make affirmations, turn off your computer, TV, or smart phone, don't eat meat, caffeine, sugar or drink alcohol or take drugs, get more sleep, notice things around you, be creative, go out in nature, trust, ground yourself, talk to yourself, do a guided meditation, visualize, think of a question and get your feelings or imagination to answer it.

These are not really good exercises specifically for intuition and probably would frustrate most people when trying using their intuition. Another real sample of a poor exercise states, "First, sit comfortably. Then begin to inhale and exhale. Concentrate on the process. After a while, try to look at the near future and see what you can see. This will take some time so keep practicing regularly." The exercise ends there. It is very vague and does not give you clear tangible steps to take.

Like learning any skill, you need to practice performing the skill that you want to improve. For example, if you're learning how to be a better tennis player, you can work with weights to improve your strength, stretch, eat better and perhaps go run to have stronger legs. But, none of those things are going to directly help you play a better tennis game. You have to actually practice playing tennis.

So, what makes a good intuition exercise? There are 5 major points that a good intuition exercise should have:

1. Be able to validate your results.

You have to be able to validate the results. This means did you get an intuitive message that was right. Was it a hit, or was it a miss? Make sure if you do any intuition exercise, that the information you pick up can be checked. It is important to know if you received your intuitive message correctly so you know when your intuition is working or not. For example, say the exercise is to use your intuition to pick up what someone had for lunch yesterday. If you choose that someone to be your favorite movie star you may not be able to check later if you were right or not, unless you can actually contact your favorite movie star and ask them. If you chose your spouse to use your intuition to pick up what they had for lunch yesterday, you would certainly be able to validate whether your intuition was right or not.

This also helps you experience what it is like when your intuition is right. Just as you learn how to serve the tennis ball into the service box, you can see right away if what you are doing is working or not. You can remember what it felt like as you hit the ball, precisely how you stood and held the racket. That helps you repeat what you had done that works. With intuition, when you get a hit, you can remember what it was like to receive a correct intuitive hit.

Remember, don't practice tennis in the dark. If you are doing an exercise with a partner they need to be able to validate the intuition pop-up information you are giving them. If you are doing a remote viewing exercise with your partner and she gives you a place to remotely view where she's never seen or been to before, she won't be able to validate any information you give her.

2. Practice on something simple, not emotional and not important.

There is a big temptation to start using your intuition on important life problems or decisions about your health, relationships or money. Don't practice your intuition on these kinds of big decisions. All the practice to build your intuition skill prepares you to use your intuition on the big stuff after you've reached a comfortable level. You've just learned a new technique and now you have to use it on simple exercises. The technique is important but it is not enough. You need to practice. This is similar to learning how to ski where in the beginning you just got off the "bunny slope" and you've made it down the beginner green trail a couple of times, but you're a long way from getting on the advanced double black diamond trail.

Emotional subjects bring in your fears, doubts and your thinking mind. These are all enemies of being able to receive your intuition clearly. Practice your intuition on non-emotional things that are simple and not important. That way you can focus on learning how your intuition works inside of you rather than struggling to separate your thinking mind from your intuition on big decisions. The exercises listed here are good examples of simple and non-important types of subjects you can start to practice with.

Right now you're practicing the experience of your intuition so you can notice her when she is communicating with you. As you practice you may surprise yourself by finding out that your intuition is sharing information with you all the time in ways you didn't realize. Here's how I found out that my intuition does just that and answers my thoughts very quickly just by practicing.

Visiting a doctor that I had been seeing every few months, I found myself wondering how he was doing while waiting for him to come in the examining room. On my last visit I found out that he was having a health issue. I realized it was the perfect opportunity to practice by asking my intuition about his health. Instantly, an image of him popped up in my mind of him hunched over on crutches wearing a striped green and white shirt. The images shocked me and I reflexively thought, "Oh, don't think like that, that's a terrible thing to think." So I pushed the picture out of my mind. Then using the intuition technique I paused, asked my angels permission to send me a message for our highest good, through my intuition, on how my doctor was doing.

I received some intuitive messages and then waited. Then when my doctor came through the door, he was hunched over on crutches wearing a green and white striped shirt! I was stunned having forgotten my initial pop-up image. Realizing that I had "seen" him in a quick pop-up image but dismissed it immediately because I was conditioned to not think "bad" thoughts of people, this was a revelation to me.

From this exercise, I learned that I receive intuitive pop-up images or pictures in my mind very quickly in response to a question I was merely thinking of asking my intuition, but hadn't formally asked yet. This taught me two invaluable things to remember: first, that intuition is listening into our thoughts and can be triggered to respond any time; second, that intuition's pop-up messages can be fleeting, very quick and subtle. What made this even more significant is that I experienced what quick and subtle intuitive pop-ups felt like for me.

Simple exercises perfect your knowing what intuition is like for you. As you practice more and more you'll experience true intuitive messages that you've validated. You will know exactly when your intuition occurred and where you correctly received it. This is the way you build trust in your ability to know when you have correctly received a message from your intuition. The only way you can clearly experience intuition without interference from your thinking mind and Ego is to practice on small and unimportant things.

3. Remember what you received by writing it down.

When you are doing an intuition exercise and you are collecting your intuition pop-ups, the best thing to do is to write them down. There are several reasons for this. When you write down what you believe you are receiving from your intuition, you are less likely to judge what you receive. It is very important not to edit what you are getting. Everything you feel, see, hear or think inside your mind or outside of you can be an intuitive pop-up. Writing them down captures what you received and frees you up from having to try to remember what you have gotten. You don't have to write in great detail, you can just take notes. The act of writing is in itself a way of channeling intuitive messages as well. You can feel free to doodle or draw pictures if your intuition moves you to do so. When you receive your intuition pop-ups you can write them as a list on your paper.

Remember do not edit what you receive, just write it down. Sometimes you may find you have to prevent yourself from judging or editing what you are writing. Editing is your Ego and thinking mind getting in the way. Try to ignore the urge to edit. As you write, your thinking mind will be judging in the background, which is normal. As you write something down you may find yourself second-guessing it, thinking, "Oh, that can't be right. I'm making this all up. That seems crazy." Let your second-guessing-thinking-ego-mind blabber on, but don't pay attention to it. Just keep writing.

4. Have a technique or method to practice.

A technique is a set of stepwise procedures to complete a task. It is similar to a recipe for cooking. The technique should be tangible. One of the very frustrating things I had found in studying how to use intuition is the vagueness that comes in many books and intuition classes. You often hear that to use your intuition you have to "go into your heart" or "connect to spirit"; often skipping the entire process of how to do it and then follow up with "after you've received your intuitive message…" — all of which is baffling. The intuition technique here is the cycle of Ask, Be Open, Collect, and Do It Again, which should be quite clear. Coupled in this technique is understanding the variety of ways intuition pop-ups can come to you for you to collect. This is detailed out in previous chapters.

5. The technique should have steps to follow.

Using a technique or method that has easy clear steps you can follow is key to being able to practice using your intuition over and over again. With intuition you need a technique to make your intuition happen on command, and then how to receive and interpret your intuitive messages.

A technique will allow you to entrain inside you a stepwise process that you will do automatically after having practiced it often. Eventually, with practice, you'll become comfortable asking your intuition a series of many questions, being in the open state to receive and then collecting many intuitive pop-ups, which will form the intuitive message with detail for you.

Those are the 5 major points a good intuition exercise must have. In summary, they are:

1. Be able to validate your results.
2. Practice on something simple, not emotional and not important.
3. Remember what you received by writing it down.
4. Have a technique or method that you practice.
5. The technique should have steps to follow.

The Best Way to Do an Intuition Exercise

You can do intuition exercises on your own or practice with a partner. If you can practice your intuition exercises with a friend, or a classmate, or someone who'd like to practice with you, that's better than doing exercises on your own. This is because there's more you can validate with another person than when you're by yourself. You can practice with someone you know well like a family member or someone you don't know such as a fellow student in a class. Even though you think you may know too much about a friend or a family member to be partner, it may surprise you that there is still quite a bit you won't know about them. Friends can still be good practice buddies.

Choose a partner of like-mind who is not going to compete with you. You can pick someone who is just learning like you are. Also, it's important to practice with someone you are comfortable with. You both have to be able to be open and relaxed, and not afraid to have a "miss" because that's how you learn and improve.

How you do your intuition exercise practice affects how quickly you will progress. These five steps are especially important when you are working with a partner. By following these five steps you can avoid the pitfalls of doing your intuition exercises improperly.

1. Be brave.

You're going to be uncomfortable when you first start out and it's going to feel like you don't know what you're doing. That's all okay. It's a new experience. You also may have performance anxiety. To help yourself be brave and fix this, stick to an intuition technique, which has a step-by-step process. That way it becomes easier to do, and not be nervous. If you're really nervous or you feel you're thinking too much, you can use an intuition tool from what I call your Intuition Toolkit.

I teach both the Intuition On Demand Technique and toolkit because combined they help you focus on a stepwise process and use tools to get you out of your Ego mind. My mother was a master voice teacher and often had to work with her students to get over stage fright and nervousness. She always said that if you are nervous just focus on your technique, that process with steps that you could rely on. I learned another great technique to get over the anxiety, which was from my college math teacher who was an expert on math anxiety. He always taught us to start solving a math problem with "What is the first thing you do?" meaning the first step and that got you over the hump of getting going. In the Intuition On Demand Technique the first thing you do is ask a question.

Nike's slogan, "Just do it," is good to keep in mind, or what my intuition teacher would say is to, "Blah it out" as she made a face as if she were spitting something out. The next best instruction she gave was, "Don't edit anything." In her class, in the first hour of the first day, she asked us to do a reading for a randomly picked classmate. She said, "Okay, you're all going to do a reading for each other, are you ready?" We all shook our heads "no" but she reassured us that we were ready. I was a bit nervous as I sat in front of my partner who was a young happy-looking woman named Robin. Our task as a new student Angel Reader was to get a message from our sitter's angels and pass it on to them. I followed the process our teacher gave us, and immediately received, "Tell her not to worry about her health, she'll be okay." I was a bit hesitant. Did I really get this as a message? Could it be right? She doesn't look sick! Did I make it up? But, remembering my teacher's words, "Don't edit anything," I just told Robin what I got. "The angels told me to tell you not to worry about your health, you're going to be okay." Suddenly, Robin burst into tears. I said, "Are you okay?" She replied, "Yes,…I was just told I have cancer."

Needless to say, I was very surprised. Long story short, she ultimately was okay and is well and healthy now. But, the reason I tell the story is because the experience really stuck in my mind of how important it is to not edit what you get. A student just the other day told me how she loves one of the keys I teach, "You get what you get and you don't get upset."

2. Write it all down.

This is a very important step. Don't skip it. Write down everything you receive as your intuition pop-ups. Get something to write with and write on, using the old fashioned pen and paper or use your smart phone or computer. Create a list of the pop-ups and include everything you feel, see or hear and remember, don't edit anything.

Only share with your exercise partner what you received after you've gotten everything you can from your intuition for the exercise. You'll often know there is no more to receive because your pop-ups just seem to stop coming on their own. The reason you write everything down is you are less likely to edit what you are writing compared to speaking out loud to someone what you are receiving. Writing also prevents the reader from being negatively influenced by a sitter saying, "no." Even if you have some experience reading for someone else, it is a good practice to write all of your intuition pop-ups. You'll see why when we go over sharing your pop-ups with your partner.

My best intuition hits were things I thought were just absolutely crazy and absurd. Writing down what I was receiving saved me from editing away those hits before I knew they were accurate. I was doing a reading to pick up intuitive information about a person named Jay for my sitter. As a new reader, I was just starting to get more intuitive pop-ups as pictures, so I was not too confident in the images that appeared in my mind. In this case, one of the pop-ups was an image of white Adidas running shoes with red stripes on the side, but the shoes were grey from what looked like over use. As I wrote what I saw in my mind, my judging mind thought, "This is ridiculous, I'm making all of this up." But I stuck with it and told my sitter what I received. She laughed and then validated that Jay used to have an old pair of Adidas running shoes that had red stripes on the side. He had worn them so much and so long they were all grey and worn out. Apparently, the shoes became an inside joke with his friends who would tease him about the shoes and tell him to throw them away.

I was very glad I wrote everything down which allowed me to not edit or reject what I thought was ridiculous or judge what my intuition was giving me.

3. Share your list of what you received 2 or 3 items at a time.

This is an important step, so please make sure you follow this step properly. After you believe you've received everything you could, you can share with your partner what is on your list. Go through your list slowly and share only 2 or 3 things at a time. Don't rush through your list even though you'll want to. There is a strong natural desire to give everything on your list quickly, hoping that you'll have some hits. You have to resist the desire to rush. Give your partner time to think and see if they are "hits" or not. You may be surprised that things you think are misses, are actually right on! At the same time, don't try to make everything you received fit, or force it to have meaning. As you go through your list don't judge yourself, just share it honestly. Remember this is all practice! Your partner can respond to what you share with a "yes that's right," "no" or "maybe." Get through your list and then your partner can share more fully what they feel are hits, going back and telling you more detail.

For each item that is a hit, I strongly suggest that you put a star or a check next to it. This is because it will reinforce in you the times and items where you correctly received your intuition messages. You can also celebrate in your mind. One of my favorite masterful psychic mediums would do a mini celebration like a little girl every time she had a hit. It was really cute to watch since her demeanor was generally very serious. So don't be afraid to celebrate your hits, and ignore your misses. You want to reinforce when you do well so you can do it again. When you write it down, it helps you remember how the intuitive hit came to you.

I also suggest that if you have an intuitive success any time during your day, that you go home and write it down as a story. This will also reinforce how you received the hit, and will help you remember details of exactly how your intuition comes to you. You may even realize that your intuition gave you more information than you first noticed. Perhaps the image had more detail than you first thought or that you had other intuitive pop-ups that came along with the one you wrote down but didn't note it. This all builds your intuition knowledge, skill and experience so you can more easily notice when your intuition comes to you again.

Writing your pop-ups down also gives you a written collection of when your intuition was working well. This builds your trust in your intuition and gives you confidence that you really can do this!

4. Remember, intuition comes in symbols and pieces.

Remember, your intuition speaks in symbols and in pieces. You may have to expect that your pop-ups may be symbols. What you receive intuitively could be pieces of the full meaning, so it is important to go through everything you received. That is why the third step in the technique is Collect. As you go through the cycle of Ask, Be Open, Collect over and over you will get more pop-ups that present themselves. At some point the pop-ups will show themselves as parts of a bigger picture and the meaning will be apparent. Remember, don't stretch the meaning or try to make up a meaning.

5. Don't get down on yourself.

During the exercise, when you share what you received it is very important to not get down on yourself. In particular, don't let your energy drop, as one of my mentors told me. What it means to drop your energy is to stay light and move on. When your sitter says, "No" you can just say, "Thank you" and move on to the next thing on your list. Don't let yourself be too disappointed because this is all practice so know that you are going to have some misses, but it's okay. Just like learning a sport like tennis, if you're practicing how to serve the ball and you hit it out of the court, you just pick up another ball and try again. It's the same with your intuition. Just let it go. If you have a miss just move on. That's how to really exercise your intuition well!

In summary, the best way to do an intuition exercise is to keep these steps in mind:

1. Be brave.
2. Write it all down.
3. Share your list of what you received 2 or 3 at a time.
4. Remember, intuition comes in symbols and pieces.
5. Don't get down on yourself.

What Not to Do in an Intuition Exercise

The first thing you do not want to do during an intuition exercise is to start guessing. If you find your mind is thinking, "Maybe it's this, or maybe it's that," you're guessing. You will get something from your intuition because you are always seeing, feeling and hearing.

Another common problem people have is they try to make everything fit. If it doesn't fit, don't try to force it to fit. Remember, you don't know what the message is because it's not coming from you. If you don't get the message yet, then you have to keep going through the Q&A cycle in the technique to get more intuition pieces.

Another big mistake is to use an exercise on something that you cannot validate. For example, you may be picking up intuitive information about a stranger, but because you don't know them you generally can't ask them to find out if you were right or not. Don't try to use your logic and deductive powers to figure out the intuition message. The message should be readily apparent from the collection of pop-ups you have received. If you are still receiving pieces that don't make sense, then let them go.

Give yourself a break and don't be impatient. It takes time to develop any skill and is the case with intuition. You may have some amazing hits once and a while in the beginning, and then you may have a dry spell. Keep going and practice often by keeping it simple. You are practicing to receive small pieces of information that can be validated. You're not going to be able to get deep detailed information in the beginning. Don't give up.

Why Do Misses Happen?

There are many reasons why we don't pick up our intuitive messages accurately. The obvious one is that our mind chatter gets in the way of receiving our messages clearly. What should you do with information you think is intuitive that you cannot immediately validate? Just hang on to it and don't "dis" it. This means don't discount, dismiss or discredit it. There are other possibilities for why misses occur. As a sitter or an intuitive reader, either during a practice session or in the public, it is important to keep the following in mind. Here are the top four reasons why misses occur that happen most frequently:

1. You're looking for your intuition to give you an answer that you are expecting or desperately want. We often may be looking for a

particular answer or have a certain perspective of a situation that limits us to what the meaning of the information is.

2. You misinterpret what your intuition is telling you. By the same token, don't try to stretch the meaning too far, because if it doesn't feel like a fit, then that's not it. Many times the meaning will come to us much later.

3. You are getting information you may not expect or know about and it may be hard to understand. This is because many things can occur. The meaning may not be readily apparent to you. Messages and meanings come from a wide perspective, and sometimes they are answering a different question than you asked. There may be something that comes up that we are unfamiliar with. It is similar to talking to someone. You don't know everything they know and they may tell you something you didn't know. Many times, family members, or friends help you understand the message because there may be a connection or meaning they see that you don't.

4. The message may have something to do with the future, something that has not occurred yet.

Go Forth and Practice

There is a lot here that covered intuition exercises and the most effective way to do them. It is important to keep in mind the points made here so that you can improve your intuitive skills exponentially. *Keep in mind if you just rush into the exercises and don't pay attention to the key points of how to do them, you'll just get frustrated.* You will see marked improvement by practicing your exercises properly. The next chapter will give you exercises you can do by yourself as well as with a partner and how to use your intuition gradually for your everyday life decisions. Now go forth and practice, practice, practice!

Highlighted Tips and Summary

A good intuition exercise involves the following:

1. Be able to validate your results.
2. Practice on something simple, not emotional and not important.
3. Remember what you received by writing it down.
4. Have a technique or method that you practice.
5. Have a technique that has clear steps to follow.

The best way to do an intuition exercise:

1. Be brave.
2. Write it all down.
3. Share your list of what you received 2 or 3 items at a time.
4. Remember, intuition comes in symbols and pieces.
5. Don't get down on yourself.

What not to do in an intuition exercise:

1. Don't guess.
2. Don't try to make everything fit.
3. Do not practice on something you cannot validate.
4. Do not use your deductive reasoning to figure out the intuitive message.
5. Give yourself a break and don't be impatient.

CHAPTER 12

Intuition Exercises to Practice and How to Apply Your Intuition to Life – Money, Love, Health

• • • • • • • • • • • • • •

The biggest improvement you'll make with your intuition will come after you exercise and practice using your intuition muscles!

Intuition Exercises to Do Alone

It may surprise you that you can use your intuition for many mundane things in your daily life that are actually excellent intuition exercises. Intuition is not meant only to provide profound life-saving or life-changing messages. Your intuition is active all the time and is with you at your beck and call any time you need assistance or just information. You can take advantage of this to create intuition exercises for yourself. Below is a sample of intuition exercises that you can try by yourself and then feel free to make up your own. The possibilities are endless!

Notice that the exercises will help you practice where you can validate your results and see if what you picked up was correct. Remember it's all just practice! You get what you get and you don't get upset, just keep practicing and you will get better.

Where Is That Person Going?

If you're out driving or walking, you can exercise your intuition to see where someone in front of you is going to go. For example, if you're driving behind someone use your intuition to predict where they will go. Will they turn left or right? Where will they exit? When will they turn? Will they be in front of you the entire way to your destination? I came up with this one when I was behind someone who was driving very slowly and I was getting impatient wondering when I was going to be free of their impeding me getting to where I was going.

A couple of ways you can do this is by first asking your intuition "Where is this person going to go or turn off?" Then imagine you are continuing on your journey and in your mind feel or "see" where they are no longer in front of you.

Feeling Energy Of People And Places

Your intuitive sense of feeling is constantly on and sensing changes and shifts in the energy around you. This is particularly true for sensing the energy coming from another person. It is easier to feel other people's energy when you are outside your home because home is where the energy is familiar and relatively stable. As you move closer to people the feeling of their energy will be stronger, especially if they are in a highly emotional state. That can be a state of fear, anxiety, anger, frustration, love, happiness, excitement or joy. You can pay attention to how your physical and emotional feelings shift slightly when people are near or pass by you. Of course you have to be aware of how you're feeling first.

Sometimes these subtle changes make you feel a little tense, warm, perhaps a bit ill, uncomfortable, loved, or even buzzy. Walk towards and then away from the place or person where your feelings changed. If the feeling gets stronger when you move forward and then lessens or goes away when you walk away from the person or place, you know it's them and not you that caused the feeling. This is one way you can validate your intuition sensing the energy.

I experienced this shift quite noticeably once in a restaurant. Entering I felt fine as we waited for our table. After being seated at our table I immediately felt a bit dizzy and buzzy. I suspected it might have been the lighting because it seemed a bit bright there, so I put my hands over my eyes. The feeling didn't change and it was still there. I've learned that whenever I have a change in my feelings out of the blue like this I review in my mind if it could be me, and if not, I check my surroundings to see if it is someone or something else. It wasn't me because I was feeling fine all day and hadn't done anything out of the ordinary. I scanned the tables around us and intuitively I felt that the energy that was causing my dizziness and buzzing was coming from a pair of elderly couples in front of us. The only way I could validate if it was those couples at that table was when they left before us and the feelings went with them. I was back to being calm and feeling good again!

Help Make Small Decisions

You are always making small decisions. These are great opportunities to use your intuition and then see if your intuitive choice was a good one. This is especially good to do when you have a choice of two things that you're having a tough time deciding which to choose. In a restaurant: can't choose between two dishes on the menu that look really good to you? Use your intuition. Ask your intuition which one will taste best and feel great in your stomach. See which one it leads you to and then when you have the meal you chose, your validation is whether your meal was something you really enjoyed. I have found choosing a menu item this way has often led to amazingly delicious meals. Sometimes it's further validated when my husband chooses the other dish at the same time and I get to taste both and I discover the one my intuition chose tasted better to me. You can do the same, for which item to buy, which store to go into and so on.

One weekend, attending my cousin's wedding, I had brought white satin pumps to wear with a long dress. I didn't know that the wedding was going to be held outside in soft grass. I quickly realized my pumps would sink in the soft ground and probably ruin them, which would not be good. Having barely enough time to run to a nearby mall I went to see if I could find something else to wear. I'd never been in the area before and had no idea where to look. I am not really good with fashion and am more of a sneaker gal. I asked my intuition to help me find the right store. Descending down the escalator, I spied a shoe store on my right and felt drawn to go inside, but looking at the store display, the shoes were very glitzy and exotic. There were stilettos, boots with super high heels and sequins, and platform shoes. I thought, "I'll never find something that fits me or looks right there." Running out of time, I had no choice and I went with my intuition. Quickly walking through the store, my eye caught one pair of flat sandals with a white decorative leather over the top, which looked just dressy enough for my dress. Very nice and they were on sale!

Predict The Future Exercise

Your intuition can assist in predicting the outcome of events like elections, races, sporting events, and so on. Just ask your intuition the question, "What will the final score be?" or "Who will win?" See what intuitive pop-up you receive immediately. Though the future isn't fixed there are energetic trends that you can tune into. If your prediction is wrong, don't give it too much weight. You are tapping into general trends of energies to predict the events that may occur in the future.

What Time Is It?

You don't have a watch or you're not near a clock? The next time you want to know the time, before you look at the time on a device, see if you can use your intuition to pick up what the time is. Ask your intuition to give you the time, see what pops up first in your head. You may see an analog or a digital clock. Then you can check to see if you're right.

When Will I Be Called, Or Be Next In Line?

It seems like we spend lots of time waiting in a queue, line or waiting to be called next. Places you'll be waiting are grocery stores, the post office, a government office to get your driver's license, passport, etc. Another long wait could be in a doctor's office. In any case, we never really know exactly when we'll be called in or be served. This is a great opportunity to practice your intuition to predict when you'll be called in to be served. Your intuitive pop-up may be an image of an analog or a digital clock or you hear the number of minutes you'll wait. Just ask your intuition, "When will I go in to be served?"

Magazine Intuition Exercise

You can use your intuition to pick up the characteristics of the photograph that is on the last page of the magazine. Get a magazine that you haven't read before. Then ask your intuition to give you information about the photograph on the last page. You may have a feeling, or a color, or hear a word and you also receive an image. Then check if what you received matches the picture or even the words that are on the last page.

Pre-Meeting Information About Someone

If you're going to meet a friend or someone you don't know later in the day, ask your intuition for information about them. For example, what are they wearing today, or perhaps what is their mood like today? You may ask your intuition to give you personality traits of a person you'll meet for the first time.

Help Me Find What I'm Looking For!

Can't find what you want in the store, or trying to find that new restaurant and you don't have GPS? Perhaps you're looking for a particular item in a store but don't know where it is. Use your intuition to guide you. Archangel Chamuel is the angel who helps you find lost things and you can call on him to help you by sending you a message through your intuition. Just ask him to show you, through your intuition, where the item you seek is.

Which Elevator Will Arrive Next?

The next time you need to get on an elevator and there are several at the elevator bank, use your intuition to tell you which one will arrive first. Once you are on the elevator, ask your intuition which floor other passengers are going to get off at before they hit the floor button. Keep in mind that you may not get a specific number, but you may receive whether they get off before you, or after you.

Who Will Serve Me?

Ever get on a single line at the bank, airport check-in station or at the department store that feeds into a row of tellers, agents or cashiers? Ask your intuition which teller, agent or cashier you will be going to.

Another variation of this is to use your intuition to pick up how many or who will be in a class or meeting that you regularly go to. If you take a class regularly, like a Yoga class or even going to church, you never know how many people or who will show up. Use your intuition to see how many people will arrive, and even who that you know will be there. You can also ask your intuition how many men and women will attend.

Predicting Arrivals

To predict when someone will arrive, such as a guest, your spouse, or a stranger in a public place, see if you can use your intuition to receive the time of arrival. You can also try to predict when they are going to leave! Some people you just don't want to be around. During my week's stay in the hospital because of a heart infection I shared a room with a very impatient and crotchety old woman. For her, the food was inedible, the light was too bright or too dark and the room was too cold. Every few minutes she called the nurse to complain. Even though she had extra blankets brought in, she requested that they turn up the heat. It was so hot in the room the nurses would come in and say, "Why is it so hot in here?" I couldn't rest and she was making me very uncomfortable. I asked my angels, "What is up with this woman? How long is she going to be here?" Through my intuition they told me, "She doesn't need to be here, she's leaving tomorrow." And sure enough, she left the next day!

News Headlines

Teaser headlines in the news are good for practicing your intuition. When you see news headlines that don't give you much information, use your intuition to tell you what the story is about; the details and what happened. For example, a news headline like, "Daring Rescue of Four People Trapped in Car – News at 6." You can ask your intuition about the four people: How many were adults and/or children? How many were female or male? What kind of car was it? Why did they need to be rescued? Can you pick up details of the scene of the incident? You can then validate your answers when the news story is reported later or you can read about it by searching online.

Intuition Exercises to Do with a Partner

All of the tools in your Intuition Toolkit, described in a previous chapter, can be used as intuition exercises with a partner. Let's put the pieces together on how you would use the tools in the Intuition Toolkit and the proper way to do an intuition exercise using an example. Below are the two checklists of what a good intuition exercise is and what to do when you are doing the exercise with someone else. Let's review. A good intuition exercise requires that you:

1. Be able to validate your results.
2. Practice on something simple, not emotional and not important.
3. Remember what you received by writing it down.
4. Have a technique or method that you practice.
5. Have a technique that has clear steps to follow.

Example Intuition Exercise Using a Tool from the Toolkit –
A Photograph of Someone

This is an example of how to use a tool from your Intuition Toolkit. You can use other intuition tools in a similar way. To do this exercise you can get together with your practice partner who may be a friend, family member or someone in your intuition development circle. It is best to pick someone you don't know but if you do know your partner, well that is fine. Each of you participating in the exercise should bring a photograph of someone else you know well, who your partner doesn't know. One of you will be the sitter, which is the person being read and giving the reader the photograph. The reader will be looking at the photograph and writing down intuitive information they pick up about the person in the photograph.

STEP-BY-STEP

1. The reader will take the photo and focus on the person in the picture.
2. The reader will ask their intuition to get a message from your guides and angels, "Tell me about this person, what do I need to know about her or him?"
3. As a reader, look at the photo and pay attention to what you immediately feel from the person's face. Notice your physical and emotional pop-ups as you look at the photograph.
4. The reader can ask their intuition these questions about the picture: How is this person related to the sitter? What is this person's personality like? Where do they live? Is there a message your guides and angels want the sitter to know about this person?

As readers receive intuition pop-ups from these questions write them down in a list format. Write until you feel there is nothing more to receive. Write what first comes to you and do not edit anything. It may be feelings, or images, write those too. It's important that you don't rationalize what you're looking at, nor be misled by clothing, or others in the photograph. Don't share what you received yet. Now you can switch roles as sitter and reader.

Once both of you have had a turn at reading each other's photographs then you can share. This is important for beginners because if your partner is a reader first and shares with you what they received, you may consider some of them to be amazing hits. That can be very intimidating if you now have to take your turn at reading their photograph. This is why it is important for both of you to take your turns and write down your intuition pop-ups first. Then once both of you have read each other's photograph you can then share. Remember these steps when you are receiving your intuition pop-ups and then share your list of pop-ups:

1. Be brave.
2. Write all of your pop-ups down, don't edit.
3. Share your list of what you received, two or three items at a time, slowly! Allow your sitter to make the connection with your pop-ups.
4. Remember, intuition comes in symbols and pieces.
5. Don't get down on yourself.

IMPORTANT REMINDER: The most important part of the exercise is seeing what things you received were misses and which were hits. Don't get down on yourself when it comes to misses. Just let them go. This is the hardest part for everyone for some reason. Missing does not mean you cannot do this, and it also does not mean you're not good at it. This is all practice. Just like practicing how to hit a ball with a bat in baseball, if you miss the ball, you just try again. You don't give up, you get another ball and try again. By the same token, you should celebrate your hits. "YES!!! I got it!" is a good way to think when you have a hit. Then put a check mark or a star to indicate that one on your list is a hit. It is vitally important you remember these things because I have found it is where most students have problems or even forget their hits. This is the place where you are actually doing the deep learning and conditioning your mind to recognize your intuition.

Intuition Development Groups or Circles

A development group or circle is a group of people who get together to practice their intuition for the purpose of improving by doing exercises together. Being in a development group can be very powerful in boosting your intuition skill quickly through regular practice with other people. These groups are generally led by someone who knows how to conduct a development circle. The group normally meets on a regular basis, weekly or monthly. The format of the circle activities varies greatly. Some will include meditations or energy healing during the meetings. Usually, the focus of the meeting is to do exercises to develop psychic and intuitive skills. The group may do an exercise all together as a group or pair off to do exercises.

Development Circles come in two types: closed and open. An open Development Circle is one where anyone can join and just show up. Closed Development Circles are joined by invitation only. In a closed group usually members of the group will ask a friend to join by making a request to the group leader to invite them. Also, if you are looking to get into a closed group you would have to know the group leader or someone in the group to help you get permission to join.

It is important to find an Intuition Development Circle that you feel comfortable with. These groups, especially closed circles, often have members who have been together for a very long time and form strong cliques that are not too welcoming of strangers. Open Development Circles are more welcoming though the members may come and go more frequently. Development Groups or Circles can be a great way to hone your intuition skills in a safe and comfortable environment. You will find that your skills increase to a master level faster than if you were practicing alone. I've led an Intuition Development Group for years and have watched people's intuition skills just skyrocket and at the same time have a lot of fun! You can find an Intuition or Psychic Development Circle near you or even online these days through forums or places where groups advertise such as Meetup.com.

How to Apply Your Intuition to Life – Money, Love and Health

Finally, as you get to a high level of skill with your intuition you are ready to use it on more important decisions. The major areas of our life where we make big decisions and unfortunately often involve emotionally charged situations, are Money and Career, Love and Relationships, Health and Well Being. Keep in mind that you should *NOT* use your intuition for these areas of your life if you have just started working to develop your intuition. It will be too difficult since these are highly emotional and involve intense, often fearful, feelings. You will have to have a strong sense of when your intuition is truly speaking to you so you can get a clear reliable intuitive message. Your intuition is best at guiding you but not deciding for you. Keep in mind that what you will receive from your intuition is more likely guidance rather than telling you what to do. Your thinking mind is responsible for deciding what to choose. Your intuition is just assisting you.

Using Your Intuition for Business, Money, Career or Life Purpose

One of the important areas of our lives is working to make money, whether it is a job or a career. You have lots of questions about how to get ahead or make more money such as; "Should I change my job?" "Should I take this offer?" "Is this person I'm interviewing right for the position?" "Should I go into partnership with this person?" "Will I regret it?" or "How do I deal with a difficult co-worker?" "How do I get promoted?" There are dozens of books and hundreds of articles written on using your gut instincts in business. Over and over they claim how important intuition is to highly successful people making business decisions. Sometimes there is just too much information to sort out to make an easy decision they claim and therefore rely on their intuition to decide. While there have been volumes of literature on business intuition, none talk about how to develop it or actually use it, other than to "go with what you feel." Here are some ways you can use the tools you've learned in this book to apply to business situations.

Should You Stay or Should You Go?

When making a choice between two options you can use your intuition. Some questions would be: "Should I change my job?" "Should I take this offer?" "Should I take on this new project?" Using the A/B Intuition Tool can help with your decision. To do this, you imagine that you have already chosen A first and move into the future. Then ask your intuition some questions using the Intuition On Demand Technique such as, "I've chosen A and it is now a few months into the future. What am I feeling now? What is going on around me? How are my relationships with the people involved?" See what your intuition pops up for you. Then you can do the same process but using B. Your intuition pop-ups for both A and B will probably reveal things you hadn't thought of. Another tool you can use here is the Timeline tool to see intuitively how either A or B will be in the future.

Situations Involving People

People are always a source of either pleasure or angst. Some of the questions you may be asking are: "Is this person I'm interviewing right for the position?" "Should I go into a partnership with this person?" "Will I regret it?" or "How do I deal with a difficult co-worker?" Write down the name

138

of your interviewee, co-worker, boss or whoever you want to get intuitive information about and use the Intuition Tools, using a Name or Photograph (if you have it) to find out more about the person. You can pick up personality traits, their likes and dislikes and work habits.

Life Purpose Questions

If you are looking to find out what your passion, life purpose is or asking, "How do I get promoted?" you can use the Intuitive Writing tool and ask your Intuition to give you messages for your highest good involving your life's passion or purpose. You can use the Ask For a Sign tool or use Angel Cards for a general divine message to help you find your passion, life purpose or best career choices.

Using Your Intuition for Love and Relationships

When you begin to fall in love, looking for love or have been in love for a while, emotions and fears get in the way of clearly knowing what is going on in your relationships. Our hearts and feelings take over, but that's not necessarily our intuition talking. You experience lots of confusion and mixed feelings while talking to yourself over what seems right or wrong about this guy or girl.

Maybe you started a relationship and just had your first fight. Or perhaps you've been in a long-term relationship and you have that same old argument that never seems to go away. Our emotions, wants and desires push us to go one way. Our minds tell us to do something else. We're upset and ask ourselves, "Why are they acting this way? Why don't they understand me?"

In searching for that right someone, trying to find your soul mate, you don't want to make a mistake and experience all the pain and discomfort that comes with a break-up. Where do you start looking? Or maybe someone you just met seems really into you, and you seem to like them too, but are you picking up the right vibe from them? Are they right for you? You wonder, "Am I going after them for the right reasons?" Will they be "the one." You want to make good decisions when it comes to romance.

If you're in a relationship you may be asking, "Does (s)he love me?" "Will he ask me to marry him?" "Is (s)he serious?" "Is (s)he with someone else." "How do I handle this situation in my family?" You have many Intuition Tools that can help you find out more about your significant other. For insight into people, you can use the Name or Photograph tools. You can use remote viewing to see into places and also the people in those places. The Timeline tool is great for seeing, possibly, where a relationship is going.

Using Your Intuition for Health and Wellness

Whenever you or someone you love is sick, your biggest concern is, "What's wrong with me?" "What is the best treatment for my loved one to get well?" or more commonly, "Which doctor should I use?" Even when we have minor illnesses we want to get better fast so we can get on with our lives. While these intuition techniques cannot diagnose a physical illness, you can use your intuition to pick up issues in your or someone else's metaphysical human energy system which manifests physical "dis-ease." The intuition tools you can use are energy scanning someone's body and the Timeline tool to see the outcomes of different choices.

With energy scanning you can intuitively see and feel what is going on energetically in a body. Energy healing methods usually use intuition for guidance on where to apply techniques to parts of the physical and energetic body that needs it. These techniques can help you know where your physical issue may be focused.

As far as getting assistance from your intuition on which path to take with a particular treatment or doctor here are some specific tools you can use. The Name and Photo intuition tools can give you intuitive information about a person that can help you make a decision. You can also use a Timeline tool to receive intuitive insight on which choice of treatment would have a more positive trend.

PART FOUR

Intuition Inside and Outside of Us

CHAPTER 13

What Is This "Psychic Energy" Thing? The Metaphysics of Intuition

· · · · · · · · · · · · ·

When you begin to study intuition development, you'll often hear about "psychic energy" which can leave you a bit stumped and wondering, "What is psychic energy and how do I use it with intuition?" The energy is not, per se, psychic or special in any way, but is part of the energetic system that makes up all things. You can and always do pick up information from that energy which has information that you can understand. This is what has come to be known as "psychic energy."

Energy is said to make up everything, both physical and non-physical. It is this energy that connects us to the world around us. According to physics, energy cannot be created nor destroyed, it can only be transformed, therefore all things are made of the same substance, which is Universal Energy, but is just converted into different forms. Psychic energy is a form of energy you can experience but science has not yet found an accepted way to measure it.

Albert Einstein, the great physicist, proved that energy and matter, or physical things, are the same. His famous theory $E = mc^2$ states: "E," or energy, equals "m," or mass, times a very large number, in this case it is the speed of light "c," squared. Again, both physical and non-physical things are made of energy and, in fact, all things can be seen as a continuum of the same energy.

What Psychic Energy Is

If everything is made up of energy, then what exactly is psychic energy? The oldest study of energy actually began with the Chinese about 5,000 years ago and they call the energy Qi or Chi. QiGong is a practice of working with and using this energy. QiGong literally means "energy work." Through the Daoist theory of how the Universe functions, the ancient Chinese masters developed an understanding that everything is connected energetically and even though energy may be expressed in different forms, all that exists is energy. From this Daoist philosophy the Chinese developed QiGong, which is a practice of how to work with energy based on a theory of how energy manifests into physical and non-physical form giving rise to mind, body and spirit.

Thoughts and consciousness are made of the same energy that makes up physical things. The Chinese believe that Qi or Chi is a continuum of energy that manifests both physical substance as well as subtle or non-physical things, such as consciousness and thoughts. All of this energy is one substance or thing, which could be considered Universal Consciousness or God. This energy carries information that we can pick up, process and understand conceptually. This is how we receive psychic or intuitive information, not just information from people's thoughts, but also information about everything.

Psychic energy is referring to the energy that you tap into with your intuition to gain information about people, places, things, thoughts and more. It is this subtle energy that you can access not only with your intuition but also with your mind and body. It is this energy that you can feel physically. It's not just feeling the heat from a fire, or a cool breeze but being able to feel energy that emanates from consciousness, thoughts, and other known and probably unknown things in the Universe.

It is believed that the energy that comprises everything, including you and your body, first forms as an energy grid and then from that grid the physical forms. The energy grid continues to exist along with the physical form. In the case of your human body, you have an energy grid that formed your body and still exists as part of your human energy system. This energy grid has many layers that lie one within the other like Russian dolls or like an egg, only the inner layers extend through the outer ones. Some people can see and feel this layered system, which is called the aura. The energy grid is called the human energy system.

The Human Energy System and Intuition

The human energy system is comprised of energy that makes up both the physical body as well as the consciousness. The energy of the physical body is comprised of energy fields that can be measured as electromagnetic fields called "L-Fields." The energies that comprise our thoughts and consciousness are subtle energies that never become physical but move and exist as fields of energy called the "thought field" or "T-field" (Dale 2009, 116). These T-field energies flow along the same pathways as L-Fields do, within, into and out of, the human energetic system. Energy flows through our energetic system via pathways called meridians or nadis within the framework of our physical bodies, as well as through our extended energetic field outside the boundary of our physical body, through portals or channels called chakras. Different chakras are associated with channeling different kinds of psychic information, though the processing of the meaning of this information is not in the chakras but is interpreted by the brain.

Energy from our environment, which is not limited to just our immediate vicinity but goes beyond time and space, is interacting with our own personal human energetic system. We take in energy from around us, as well as sending energy out through our chakras. The flow of energy cycles through our energetic and physical bodies is similar to the circulatory system of our blood, the difference is that the energetic system is not a closed system the way our blood flows in our bodies. It is an open system where energy is exchanged with the energy outside of our bodies. According to the Chinese, energy flows into our bodies by entering a point at the top of our heads, which takes in heaven energy and from the earth through the bottom of our perineum. This energy then fills something called the Tai chi Pole, also known as our Energetic Core, which is located along the center of our bodies slightly in front of our spine. They also believe that energy enters our Tai chi Pole through the rest of the chakras that are in our energetic body. Chakras, again, act as portals for energy to flow into and out of our energetic systems.

The energy in our Energetic Core then flows into the three Dantians and fills them like deep wells or pools of energy. These three Dantians actually encompass the seven chakras in our body. Energy is then held there to be redistributed through both the physical and energetic body via the nervous system, endocrine system, organs, blood for the physical body and the energy channels and collaterals which are the meridians of the energetic body. Again, this flow exchanges energy with the outside world. Energy flows into the physical and energetic body and then out, nourishing both of them. (Johnson 2000, 103). Though the Chakras and Dantians that are above the heart level tend to have more psychic powers associated with them, all Chakras play a role in the overall functioning of psychic and intuitive skills within the human energy system.

According to the Chinese, as energy flows into our energetic system it then circulates within us, nourishing our energy where we need it and bringing in with it energetic information that we sense and interpret. Sometimes the energy we absorb is not useful to us, and in some cases may not be good for us. Physically, energy that we take in and process manifests our organs, our muscles, and all the physical cells of our bodies. The energy that manifests our physical bodies exists before the actual manifestation of the physical occurs. Energy healing works by manipulating this energy and how it flows, so the energy in us becomes balanced and whole, which in turn then becomes manifest in the physical body. Therefore, just as the life field energy created our bodies, the life field energy continues to create wellness or sickness in our bodies.

As energy is processed in the energetic body and flows into the physical body along neural pathways, it brings information up through the spinal cord, through the brain stem, or the reptile brain, to the mid-brain and then to the neo-cortex where the logical mind can process the information contained in the energetic messages. The neo-cortex is split into the two halves of the brain, which is the left half and the right half. We'll talk more about how the brain processes intuitive information in the next chapter.

Since you are always absorbing energy through your energy systems, your body receives and interprets all the energy it senses and takes in. Your energetic body has metaphysical energetic pathways that overlap the pathways of both your physical nervous and endocrine systems. Therefore, not only do you sense energy in the physical world but you sense energy metaphysically as well. This means that you can sense the subtle energy of thoughts, consciousness, and other energy that science has not yet been able to measure.

Vision Through a Metaphysical Energy Pathway

Being able to receive images through your intuition, as clairvoyance, is based on the metaphysical energetic structures in your energetic body. These structures and their energetic pathways closely overlap your visual sensory neural pathways. People who are able to see these pathways as well as the pathways being documented by the ancient masters of QiGong have empirically discovered that these energetic pathways exist. They state that the metaphysical energy enters the center of our brow and goes through our brain passing by the pituitary and the pineal gland. These glands are associated with the chakras that sense the metaphysical light energy.

Metaphysical light energy follows this path:

1. Light enters the 3rd Eye chakra at the center of your brow.
2. It then moves down the Optical nerve.
3. Then passes around your Hypothalamus.
4. Passes by the Pituitary and Pineal Gland.
5. Finally enters the Visual Cortex at the back of your head.

What is fascinating about this is the path for metaphysical light energy within the brain touches both the pineal and pituitary glands, both of which are highly sensitive to magnetic fields. The pineal gland evolutionarily in humans once was a real eye! Today, it still has cells that can detect light. The pineal gland is thought to have evolved from the parietal eye, which is an actual functioning eye in other animals such as frogs, fish and lizards. The parietal eye uses a biochemical method of detecting light rather than the way our real eyes detect light with rod or cone cells. As this pineal gland evolved from a primitive parietal eye, also interestingly called the third eye, it retained its ability to sense both light and magnetic fields. In the animals where the parietal eye still exists, it is located in the center of their brow between their eyes.

In people, there are those who can actually see auras, human energy fields, spirits and other metaphysical phenomenon. They are likely to have an ability to consciously recognize the information sent through this pathway to their visual cortex.

Your Second Brain Gives You Gut Feelings

Chinese QiGong says the Solar Plexus Chakra, which is situated two inches above your navel, is the main distribution point for psychic energies. The Solar Plexus Charka is connected to your digestive system and can be seen as a major sensing organ for subtle energy that our brain receives and interprets. The butterflies you feel in your stomach can be a message from your gut and your gut could be considered a second brain.

Scientists call this the Enteric Nervous System, which is a large bundle of nerves that controls the functioning of your digestive system. Science has discovered that this system has all the same neurotransmitters as the brain. They have also found that it processes information to a level of complexity that allows it to act independently, learn and remember. That information can be received from physical processing of food or through the metaphysical energy structures that govern that part of the body. The information our gut processes then is transmitted up to the brain where you can become aware of it.

Intuitive Feelings Begin in Your Heart

We are most strongly connected emotionally to each other through our Heart Chakras. This Chakra is, logically, centered in the middle of your chest where your heart is. Your Heart Chakra is also a connection between the physical and metaphysical worlds. There are seven main Chakras in the body that are aligned along your spine. Three of those Chakras are below the heart and are associated with the physical world. The three Chakras above the heart are associated with the etheric or spiritual world. You can pick up feelings and emotions energetically through your Heart Chakra. There may be more complex energetic information your heart can pick up and process.

The physical heart, as an independent nervous system, senses and processes information. It can make decisions and scientists have found can demonstrate a type of learning and memory. The heart secretes hormones and neurotransmitters that communicate with the body and the brain relaying information that it is processing. It can be theorized that there is metaphysical information our hearts pick up through energetic pathways that is then transmitted to our brains so we can be aware of it.

Why Energetic Health Is Important to Intuition

Now that you can see there is a very tight connection between our energetic body and our physical body, you can imagine that when our energetic body is not healthy, we can be physically unhealthy. Your entire energetic system processes energy flowing through and uses the information contained in it. When the system is not working well, such as energy being blocked or retaining negative energy, the information won't be clear and accurate. When this happens you have difficulty receiving intuitive and psychic information. For this reason, you need to maintain your energetic health.

How to Maintain Your Energetic Health

To take care of your energy you have to do some basic energy maintenance. According to Chinese QiGong and most energy healing methodologies, energetic health is maintained by bringing in energy where it is depleted, balancing out energy where there is too much or too little and getting rid of energy that is unwanted. You normally want to bring in what could be deemed "positive" energy and get rid of "negative" energy. These three steps can be termed as Build, Balance and Purge.

There are several ways you can Build your energy. First, here are some ways you'll know your energy is depleted. You may feel tired and have a lack of energy. You may feel a lack of lightness, perhaps feel down, or fuzzy headed. You may have trouble thinking clearly, or you feel out of balance.

Some of the ways to build your energy is first to use your intention and pay attention to where you focus your mind. Stay in a positive state of mind, and keep in mind as many positive thoughts as you can. You can surround yourself with more positive things, people and by going to events that make you happy. "Like attracts like," when it comes to energy and in this case your positive being and intention will attract positive energy that you will absorb. Good positive energy is associated with positive things like love, happiness, and joy.

Here are some examples:

1. You can repeat positive affirmations such as, "I see and feel my energy as beautiful, light and full of divine love," "I am love," or you can say a prayer in alignment with whatever you believe in.
2. You can create a sacred space and altar for your space, or any positive ceremony and ritual can raise your energy and the energy of the space.
3. Blessings – bless your food, your desk, home, things, etc.
4. Meditation – all kinds.
5. Read uplifting books.
6. Listen to uplifting music that makes you feel good!
7. Watch uplifting movies, shows.

Balancing your energy involves leveling out your energy fields so there is an even amount of energy throughout your field. Sometimes you may have too much energy in one area and not enough in another. It is important that your energy is free flowing, without blockages and does not stagnate anywhere. Energy flows like water in streams and rivers.

Some energy balancing activities you can do are:

1. Tai Chi – a slow form of martial art that incorporates QiGong in its movements.
2. QiGong – an ancient practice of Chinese energy healing that has movements you can do called "forms" which are good for all kinds of energy work, including building, balancing and purging.
3. Forms of Energy Healing – Reiki, Acupuncture, Integrated Energy Healing, etc.
4. Meditation – all kinds.
5. Being out in nature is very energetically healing.
6. Exercise.
7. Be physically and mentally healthy.

Purging energy is getting rid of unwanted energy. You may have too much energy, or you have negative energy, which you don't want. Purging is a way of getting rid of the energy you don't want or have too much of.
Some ways you can do this is:

1. Have an Energy Healing session.
2. Practice QiGong.
3. Take a Sea Salt Bath – Sea salt is best to use to help clear your energy. Just mix in a ½ cup of sea salt into your bath water.
4. You can clear energy by smudging which is to use the smoke of smoldering sage to move out negative energy.
5. You can use bells or singing bowls to ring a pure sound.
6. You can sing or play recordings of chanting or devotional songs that are devoted to God, light and love.

Energy Shielding

Your energetic field is similar to the volume when you listen to music. When your energetic field is loud it can overwhelm the energy of other things. If your positive energy is "louder" than the negative energy around you, you will drown out the negative energy and not be affected by it. The stronger your energy is by being healthy and full of love and positive thoughts and attitudes the less you can be affected by negative energy around you. It's just like being in a room with a group of happy people.

One down and angry person in the room would have a harder time getting them to be down and angry too.

Raising your positive energy can shield you from negative energy. Energy raising can also infuse yourself with energy that you do want which is a good thing. Again, filling your energy field with the energy you want keeps away energy you don't want. You can easily raise your energy with just your thoughts and imagining you are filling your energy field with whatever you want that is good. You can imagine pure positive energy expanding as a bubble outward from your body with a force field shield layer to protect you.

You can also just send this energy out, as positive, high vibrating divine *LOVE*. The most powerful energy is divine energy, or whatever concept you have of divinity. You can practice imagining bringing in divine energy and then sending it out into the room. I have found it can be a very effective meditation both alone and in a group. When I have led an energy raising and clearing meditation with a group of people it can be extremely power-ful as the thoughts and intentions of others amplify its power.

If you can't increase the loudness of your good positive energy when you are in the presence of negative energy, then your thoughts and intentions can create an energetic shield against the negative energy. You can do this a few ways. Imagine pulling your energy back in to yourself so it is close to your physical body and your energy will actually follow. This way it will be less affected by energy around you. You can imagine a shield, like a force field, or a wall made of steel, titanium, or diamond, around you protecting you from negative energy. The last thing you can do is physically move away from the "source" of the negative energy if you know where it is coming from.

Highlighted Tips and Summary

- Energy makes up everything.
- Your Human Energy System has its own structure comprised of rivers and streams and pools of energy throughout your body.
- Maintaining your energetic health is important for your intuition since energy is what links your intuition to the world around you.
- Building, Balancing and Purging are keys to maintaining your energetic health.
- Energy shielding can be done by amplifying the energy in you that you want, which can be love, positive thoughts or intentions.

CHAPTER 14

The Intuitive Mind: The Brain Is Designed for Intuition

• • • • • • • • • • • • •

What Is Really Going on in Your Brain?

It has been said that humans only use 10% of our brainpower, and people make the assumption that the other 90% is up for grabs, but in actuality, our entire brain is being used all the time, it is just that we are not conscious of it. We can consciously process only a small amount of what's going on in our brains because the rest of our brain is busy with keeping our body running and possibly processing information that we don't need to attend to because of where our limited attention is focused. If we were conscious of what was going on in the rest of our brain we'd probably be overwhelmed. Much of what is going on in our brain is unconscious. So what is in that other "90%"?

Your brain is really designed for intuition, you just don't know it. In studying psychobiology, I discovered the brain science behind intuition was fascinating. If you are only conscious of a small part of the information that is being processed by your brain then what is in the information that goes unnoticed? In this information processing, you could miss important information that could be considered intuition. The source of this information could be physical, subconscious, or perhaps metaphysical. Your brain is designed to be intuitive so it can run your body and manage itself in a complex world as well as run the entire internal functioning of your body to keep it going.

What are the other functions that are active in your brain? Those functions could be digesting your food, repairing and healing your cells, keeping your balance so you don't fall when you walk or bend over, or perhaps quickly avoiding a dangerous situation that you don't have time to analyze. If you were aware of all of these at the same time, you'd be drowning in a sea of information that would be chaotic and incomprehensible. Your conscious mind would not be able to handle it. You might be injured, or worse, if you took too long to think during that dangerous situation. Therefore, there are structures in your brain that work on their own to handle many things that your thinking mind does not need to be concerned with, so it can function at an "executive" level. These executive functions are comprised of mostly planning for the future, making decisions to satisfy your desires, wants and needs and dealing with day-to-day activities. The rest of what is going on in your brain goes unnoticed and takes up a large amount of your brain and nervous system power. There is a large amount of meaningful information that your brain and body is picking up that is ignored consciously. Much of this information is subconscious and you can access some of it to make conscious.

Your Brain Is Designed to Be Intuitive

Science has shown that humans really have several brains or minds in one and each one thinks very differently from the other. One mind is considered to be the logical, judging and problem solving mind that thinks in words and step-by-step procedures. The other mind thinks in abstract concepts, symbols, signs and in a "big picture" way. Another part of our brain is more primitive, handles our emotions and our fight or flight reactions along with basic instincts. All of these brain parts and "minds" are working together all the time.

Scientific research in neuroscience has determined the kinds of mental processing associated with certain parts of the brain. They have found that intuition and the characteristics of how we experience intuition are associated with either the right side of the brain or the lower sections of the brain. The lower sections of the brain are considered the "primitive" brain where their main functions are compared to instinctive processes. The functioning of the right side of the brain is associated with the kind of experiences, awareness and communication processes that are often associated with intuition.

The lower parts of the brain, called the limbic system, are not split into two parts and are considered to be the places where primitive brain functions are, such as urges of hunger, sexual arousal, motivation, the fight or flight response, basic emotions such as fear, anger, love and affection, and is also where input from your senses is initially processed. The limbic system is considered the feeling and reacting brain. Information gathered from your senses, nervous system and the lower parts of your brain move up through the nervous system and through the brain and into the neocortex for further awareness and processing. The limbic system receives and processes intuitive information that becomes what we call gut instinct, funny vibes and feelings, or your subtle intuitive urges.

If you couple the way the brain is gathering and processing information from the environment around the body with the metaphysical human energetic system that pervades and interacts with your body and brain, it is conceivable that your brain is picking up vast amounts of information that is metaphysical. The large amount of information that you are not consciously aware of is what constitutes the substance of your intuitive messages. True intuitive messages have certain consistent and repeatable characteristics that parallel and correspond to the way certain parts of the human brain and nervous system works. This may explain how it is possible to receive information without an explanation of knowing how you know it.

How to Work with Your Intuitive Brain

Once the information is in the neocortex, the two halves of the brain interpret it based on the functionality each half specializes in. Both sides of your brain work simultaneously on information that is received, but the difference is how that information is processed. The left and the right halves of your brain are separated by a physical space down the middle of your head and are literally on the left and right side of your head. The two are joined together through a large cord of nerves called the corpus callosum. In a way, the two halves of our brains are like having two different types of personalities or consciousness. The left side is making sense of the information in terms of how we generally think. The right side is more holistic and abstract. More specifically here are the characteristics.

Left-Brain Characteristics

Thinks sequentially in a linear fashion. You do A then B then C. This helps us with deductive reasoning, determining what causes a result or figuring out a solution to a problem.

1. Rational, using reason and logic to process information.
2. Organized and puts things in order.
3. Detailed, oriented and "sees the trees but not the forest."

4. Language is understood and created by the left side of the brain.
5. Judgmental and determining what is "right" versus "wrong" or "good" versus "bad."
6. Being concerned for only yourself. Egotistical, compares oneself to others.
7. Conscious – you are aware of the information in the left-brain.

Right-Brain

1. Holistic and all inclusive, seeing things as a whole: Gestalt.
2. More connected to our feelings and emotions – in fact, there seems to be more neuronal connections to the right side of our brain and our sense of physical feeling.
3. Wordless so uses symbols instead to represent information.
4. Subconscious and you are not generally aware of the information in the right-brain.
5. This side of the brain is more intimately connected to the Limbic System or lower brain functions.
6. Notices new things or a change in the big picture.
7. At peace with all that is and at one with God. Dr. Jill Bolte Taylor, a neuroscientist, experienced this when her left-brain was shut down by a stroke.
8. Very aware of the present moment and is in the "now."

The characteristics of intuition such as not having words, speaking in symbols, conveys the big picture of information, and being able to communicate through feelings parallel the characteristics of the right side of the brain. Not surprisingly, it is the right side of the brain that is associated with receiving your intuitive messages. This side of your brains works best with symbols, images, physical and emotional feelings, which are the things that intuitive messages are made of. It is then that the left side of the brain must become aware of these intuitive messages and make sense of them by realizing their understandable meaning. Information is passed back and forth through the corpus callosum between the two brain halves. The information passed may or may not be metaphysical in origin. Interestingly, in women the corpus callosum is thicker than in men. This may explain why women tend to be more intuitive than men. They are able to be more aware of the information that is in their right-brain and give conscious meaning to it with their left-brain.

While the right-brain is collecting physical world information, it can also be collecting metaphysical information as well. The right-brain receives the intuitive messages from your body and energetic field then the left-brain interprets them. You can access the intuitive information that has been gathered by your body and other parts of your brain by going back and forth between the two sides of your brain. The Intuition On Demand Technique works to get the intuitive information that you receive and collects them from the right-brain. Your left-brain triggers your intuition to pass over information by asking it a question and then collects the answers and eventually recognizes the message. You use your left-brain to tap into your intuition by getting it to respond to questions, and then the left side accumulates the symbols, pop-ups and pieces the right side is sending as answers. Eventually, enough intuitive pieces from the right-brain accumulate so that the meaning becomes apparent to the left.

The Goal – Connecting to God

One of the most amazing accounts of what the right hemisphere is actually processing when the left side goes dormant was recounted in her book, *My Stroke of Insight* by Jill Bolte Taylor. Dr. Taylor, a neuroscientist, experienced a stroke in her left hemisphere that in the process of forming a hemorrhage quieted the brain functions there and allowed the right hemisphere processing to become more conscious. In her book, she describes her experience and what it was like to have her right hemisphere speak louder than her left, giving us first-hand insight into what right-brain consciousness is. She describes the sense of oneness with everything, of being conscious of everything around her but no longer having the mental chatter in her mind. She not only experienced the feeling of being "One with the Universe," she understood it in an ineffable way.

This is similar to the experience and understanding that monks and other spiritual masters attain through their quest to become enlightened through meditation and other spiritual practices, which may work to quiet the left hemisphere and the Ego chatter. As they move along the path toward spiritual enlightenment, natural intuitive and psychic abilities arise spontaneously and ultimately become by-products of the end goal of being one with God. Apparently, the ability to connect to All That Is, or God, is within each of us in our brain. We merely have to use our conscious awareness to find it and along the way uncover our natural intuitive and psychic abilities.

Scientific Studies That Are Literally Mind Blowing

Here in the Western world we rely on scientific evidence to prove to us intuition exists. In spite of many scientific studies demonstrating the existence of intuition and psychic abilities in people, there is still lack of acceptance by society. Furthermore, most people do not believe that if you are intuitive that you can also be psychic or have extreme intuitive abilities. Nevertheless, there has been a large amount of scientific research on psychic phenomena and intuition that have produced highly significant results demonstrating that people are intuitive and psychic without knowing it. The following are some examples of the studies and their results.

Remote Viewing

Remote viewing is the ability for a person to intuitively "see" a physical location that they have never been to and describe the physical features accurately. This phenomenon is so striking because it can be easily validated with little dispute. Remote viewing was so compelling that the United States government performed studies to see if it can be used in the military. Three physicists performed the studies on remote viewing at the Stanford Research Institute (SRI). Many of these studies were done in an electromagnetically isolated chamber, meaning the tests were done where there were no external electromagnetic influences, such as radio waves or cell phone signals, etc. The United States military had carried out many experiments on remote viewing secretly to see if psychic skills could be used for defense purposes though they eventually ended the program.

One of the military experiments had a remote viewer tested by giving him only the latitude and longitude of a location on the Earth and nothing else. The remote viewer drew a sketch of what he saw intuitively of the location. The buildings and structures he drew were at the time unknown but later verified by satellite photography. The location was a secret Soviet atom bomb laboratory in Siberia. The rest of the remote viewer's description during the test was so accurate there was a concern there may have been a breach of security although an investigation by Congress found there was none.

In another experiment, the researchers wanted to see if distance was a factor in the accuracy of remote viewing. Using remote viewing another test subject was asked to draw Jupiter before the NASA Pioneer flyby occurred. He drew rings around the large planet during the experiment. This was considered to be an error until the actual pictures came back from Pioneer showing for the first time that there are rings around Jupiter.

Predicting The Future

Predicting the future or precognition is easier to measure because the results are concrete. This allows researchers to apply the scientific method more easily to testing the phenomenon. Generally, predicting the future is done by having test subjects predict the color of a light that will turn on out of a choice of four lights, or choosing what picture on a card will show up out of a selection of five cards. A random event generator determines the light or card selected to be used so neither the tester nor the person being tested knew what was going to be selected. This method is called a double-blind study, which is considered more robust since the tester cannot give any unconscious clues to the person being tested as to what the correct choice is. This kind of study had been performed many times by different researchers.

A study was done of all of these experiments looking at the results from 309 laboratory studies done in this manner over the course of 52 years. The studies included over 2 million trials and 50,000 participants. The expectation was that positive results by chance would be 5 percent, but the analysis showed that 37 percent of the studies had positive results. The probability that these results did not occur by chance is larger than 1 billion to one. This demonstrated that people have the ability to predict events and it is not due to coincidence or chance (Powell 2009).

Telepathy

Telepathy is commonly known as "reading someone's mind." While telepathy is not exactly reading someone's mind, it is more having a shared mental experience. Telepathy can be directly validated because it can be easily measured by comparing two individual experiences.

Several scientific studies have shown beyond chance that telepathy can be demonstrated between groups of people and an individual as well as between two individuals. These studies revealed that, with conscious intent, a person could send or transmit a thought or image to another person who is physically not in the same location. The studies further compared these results to a chance event that demonstrates these results would be against great odds.

Researchers discovered that by eliminating external distractions that might interfere with receiving telepathic information there was a dramatic increase in receiving information sent telepathically. They did this by using the "ganzfeld" effect, which excluded outside distractions by creating a constant visual field of color and sound. They covered each eye of the receiver with half a Ping-Pong ball, in a room with a single colored light, while also having them wear headphones that delivered a uniform noise. In this way, extraneous sights or sounds could not distract the receiver. The receiver sat in a comfortable recliner in a separate room from the sender and was given relaxation instructions. During this time the sender would look at a picture randomly chosen out of four, unbeknownst to the receiver, and asked to mentally send this picture to the receiver.

During a 30-year period conducting 88 experiments using this ganzfeld procedure 1,008 of the 3,145 trials were successful in accurately transmitting information telepathically. The results indicated a 32 percent hit rate, which was 7 percent higher than the expected 25 percent chance rate. The odds of this happening due to chance are 29 quintillion to 1, or 29,000,000,000,000,000,000 to 1 (Powell 2009, 492). By comparison, the odds of winning the power ball lottery and getting all 5 numbers, plus the power ball correct, are 175,223,510 to 1 (Powerball n.d.).

It seems like most people have experienced telephone telepathy, that is they are thinking about someone and then that person telephones them. In some cases, the person being thought about is not someone they interact with frequently or have not spoken to in a long time. Rupert Sheldrake did some studies to see how common this phenomenon is and found some surprising results. He performed two studies on this phenomenon; one was to survey 200 randomly selected people on their experiences with having someone call them who they were just thinking about and the other was to actively test if people can tell who was telephoning.

In a study called "The Anticipation of Telephone Calls," Rupert Sheldrake surveyed 200 randomly selected people in the state of California. This study was also done previously in England with similar results, demonstrating that this occurs across cultures. His results in the California survey showed that 78% of those surveyed had an experience of having someone call them who they were just thinking about, and 68% had had an experience of thinking of someone who subsequently called them who they hadn't seen for a while.

Through this survey, it is common for many people who do not necessarily consider themselves psychic or have any special intuitive powers, to have had the telepathic experience of knowing who is going to telephone them before that person actually calls.

Bringing research into the laboratory, Sheldrake then performed a study involving 63 participants over 571 test trials. The study had 1 out of 4 individuals calling someone, so there is a 25% chance that they would randomly guess correctly. The actual success rate of predicting who was going to call was 40% across all trials, which was extremely statistically significant. Another interesting result was if that a person was emotionally close to the caller they found a higher success rate in determining who is calling. This result existed regardless of physical distance since the trials included callers who were overseas (Sheldrake and Smart, Experimental Tests for Telephone Telepathy 2003).

Between the studies of the general population and their experience with the seemingly common phenomena of telephone telepathy and studies in the lab, there is strong scientific evidence to support telepathy existing in humans who don't claim to have special intuitive talents.

Intuition in Highly Successful People in Business

Intuition in business decision-making still remains highly controversial even though there has been extensive research done on the use of intuition by executives and high-level management. Even though there is controversy over what intuition is in business management, it is considered vital to how executives and senior managers make their decisions.

In research done internationally, Jagdish Parikh surveyed over 1,300 managers from around the world. The purpose of these studies was to determine how intuition is perceived and used by top and senior managers (Parikh 1994, 49). The surveys revealed that 79% of the managers use intuition in making decisions to some extent. Over 77% of those surveyed believe that intuition contributes to greater success in business. Interestingly, only 52% would openly admit that they use their intuition (Parikh 1994, 66). This shows intuition use in business decision-making is widely accepted by a majority of managers worldwide but at the same time fewer managers will openly admit to using it.

What was also revealed was what managers considered intuition to be. Much of the literature on business intuition declares intuition as the accumulation of experience. In spite of this, most managers do not define their own intuition in this way. Parikh's study showed that over 80% considered intuition to be a decision without logical or rational methods, that it is inexplicable and comes from a feeling from within, a gut feeling or sixth sense, instinct or a subconscious process. Less than 20% felt that it was a result of accumulated information or came from an integration of previous experience.

CHAPTER 15

Calling in Help: Why Believing In "More Than Me" Makes a Difference

• • • • • • • • • • • • •

Whether you believe that your intuitive information is coming from the deeper resources in your mind or it is coming from outside of you, believing you can receive assistance from "more than me" actually helps the intuition process. Two common questions students have are, "Do I have a spirit guide or guardian angel?" and, "Do I need a spirit guide?" Their concern is that to get information from divine sources you have to have a connection to a proxy or a "go-between" helper.

Believing in "more than me" helps intuition based on both a logical reasoning of how the intuitive mind works as well as assuming that heavenly guides and angels exist and can assist with divine guidance.

If You're Okay with a Little "Woo Woo," Outside of Me Helps

The problem with accessing your intuition is your thinking mind and Ego get in the way. Ego is 100% non-intuitive and using our logic to come up with answers is often the barrier to receiving clear intuitive information. We need to get out of our thinking mind and prevent our Ego from judging and corrupting the true intuition message. The left side of your brain is the logical thinking side and you want it to be quiet so you can listen to the right side of your brain, which is intuitive. The intuitive part of our brain does not process "I, me or my," instead it speaks in broader complete concept terms. This is why you won't find "I, me or my" in your intuition messages. You need to address your intuition as separate from "You" to help keep your thinking mind quiet. If you feel that your intuitive information is coming from outside of you you will automatically be more open and think less.

Couple this with the belief that through your intuition you are receiving information that is from a wiser source than yourself, intuitive messages can become stronger and increases your trust. If you truly believe you are tapping into divine wisdom that is outside of you, that is even better.

It is not required that you have any particular belief system and you certainly do not need to practice any religion. If you believe in a specific religious belief you can use that one. If you don't have a religious belief system that's fine too; you don't need one. You may be spiritual but not religious which is okay too. I personally believe all faiths lead to the same goal and along the path we are all guided and have assistance beyond what we can see. In fact, the main reason why I developed my intuition is to be more connected to that divine guidance.

What is divine guidance? Divine usually refers to Godly or "from heaven" and so divine guidance is assistance from heaven. When you feel like you've exhausted all of your mental resources trying to solve a problem you seek outside help. Receiving help from divine sources gives you solace and comfort that you will be guided for your highest good. This means that the assistance you receive from divine guidance through your intuition is unbiased and will send you in the direction you need to go. Your "highest good" is what will benefit you in all aspects of you and your life. That includes a physical, material, mental, soul, spirit and life purpose level. What you think you want may not be in your best interest for your highest good. Having trust in guidance that is for your highest good relieves you of anxiety and fear, knowing that you are on the right path no matter what happens.

People seek divine guidance from a variety of sources that they believe in. Angels are a favorite source of divine guidance and appear in almost every religion in one form or another. Heavenly guides can come as what are known as Saints, Spirit or Animal Guides, Ascended Masters, Elementals, or even the souls of people who have passed who had wisdom to pass on to you.

Are They Real?

Are they real? Maybe, but we don't know for sure. The only way you can truly believe in anything is to experience it yourself. If you believe that you are receiving angel messages and they come to you consistently and reliably, giving you the results you believe would only come from angels, then for you, angels are real. Believing "in more than me" helps you get through life's ups and downs. Building your belief system so it is part of your day-to-day life will strengthen your belief. The comfort you receive from this will grow stronger and stronger. I personally prefer to believe in "more than me" and it has gotten me through many difficult times in life. Believing in something greater than all of us and having faith that there is a wiser, all-knowing Universal Consciousness can give you comfort and hope. It relieves you of the burden of trying to be in control all the time and that when you have done all you can do then the rest of the responsibility is up to God.

Who and What You Can Connect to Through Your Intuition

There are various kinds of guides, and you can choose which ones you want to connect with. As mentioned, some examples are the conscious energy of All That Is, Angels, Animal Guides, Spirit Guides, Saints, Ascended Masters, Elementals such as Fairies, and others. We'll go over a few of these guides so you can choose which ones you'd like to start with. Guides are helpers that are all around you and are always with you in a conscious energetic form. They have agreed to be with us throughout our lifetime to help and assist us on our life's path, from the moment we are born until we return back to heaven. They are the messengers and assistants that give us the divine messages, guidance and help. They assist us in fulfilling our life's purpose and whatever it is we agreed to experience in this lifetime before we were born.

Angels

The word angel comes from the Greek word "angelos" which means messenger. Angels act as a bridge between Heaven and Earth by serving as a channel between God and the physical world. The angels who were assigned to guide you before you were born are called Guardian Angels and you have at least two with you throughout your life. They are helpers who are all around you and always with you in a conscious energetic form. They agreed to be with you throughout your lifetime to help and assist you on your life's path, from the moment you are born until you return back to heaven. They are also the messengers who give you divine messages, guidance and help from God in answer to your prayers.

Don't expect to see angels outside of you as distinct opaque three-dimensional figures with wings and halos. Most people don't see angels outside of themselves, just as intuitive visions aren't often seen physically. They often appear as an image in your mind's eye similar to a daydream or a dream at night. You often see a flash of white or colored light, like a small dot, or sparkles, or a mist. You may just see a color or you may see a full figure with wings and halos and you may even see a full figure outside of you!

What does God want for us? Why talk to angels? My angels told me the answers through Automatic Angel Writing. They said it was simply to show us the easiest path in life! In their words they said, "Angels bring messages of wisdom and truth to you, through you as you are meant to hear them. Their messages are always full of love, support and gentle guidance. When we seek what is truly within us as the words of wisdom given to us by God's messengers, we are then following the path that God has meant for us to follow in this life. It is an easier path that is full of joy, happiness and comfort."

Spirit Guides

Spirit guides are either spirits of people who have once lived or in some cases they may never have had a body. Spirit guide is a bit of a catchall phrase. A spirit guide that is someone who had passed can be a family member such as your grandmother, father, or even a cousin. Those guides can also be spirits of people you didn't know, but have some expertise in an area that you need help with. For example, there are doctor guides, writing guides, accountant guides, or even cooking guides. Some may be other beings such as higher evolved beings that are pure consciousness. Some of these guides will be with you from the beginning of your life till the end and other guides will come and go when we need them.

Your Higher Self

Your Higher Self is the expanded part of your soul that is wiser, all knowing, eternal and is your soul's higher vibration. It is considered your true or real self that has always existed as consciousness. When you are born you forget most of your Higher Self knowledge, and memories you have when you are in spirit. Because of this, it's not something you easily can identify with when you are in body. Just know that you have a higher part of your being, which is your true nature, your soul and consciousness that you can connect to because it is part of you.

God, Source, The Universe, All That Is, Higher Consciousness

God is a tough word for people, so let's keep it broad. Being infinitely curious, I once asked our priest at our church, who also has a PhD in Theology, "What is God?" His answer was, "God is unknowable." That seemed very fitting. Without trying to define God, let's say God is All That Is, which is the all-knowing consciousness that is unknowable, beyond our comprehension. God is made of energy, which makes up all things and is the vibration of love. All of these words fall very short of what God really is. Since God is in everything and is everything then God dwells within me as me. We are part of God, but we are not God. It is then conceivable that we can connect to God and perhaps God communicates to our consciousness through our intuition.

Ascended Masters

Ascended Masters are very wise beings who have either been in body and now have passed, they can be like Buddha, Jesus, Saints, Mother Mary, and so on, or those that have never been in body, like Quan Yin – the Goddess of Mercy, or Lakshmi – the Goddess of Abundance, or Ganesh – the deity who is the Remover of Obstacles. There are thousands of Christian saints and thousands more that make up the pool of Ascended Masters.

Elementals

Elementals are what some believe to be mythical creatures, but other people believe they exist. They are considered to have a slower energetic vibration than the divine high energy of angels, but vibrate at a higher level than we do in the physical. Examples of elementals are fairies, unicorns, sprites, leprechauns, elves, pixies, etc. Fairies are the angels of the earth and are assigned to protect and take care of things in nature.

Animal Guides

Animal guides or animal totems are considered to be archetypes of the energies of nature that have qualities and characteristics of animals. By connecting with the archetypal forces of nature you can call on its energies, and understand the influence of these energies in your life since there are specific ones that you are connected with.

The animals themselves have certain behavior characteristics and, in part, those signify the character of the energy that you are connecting with. For example, the Hawk animal guide is a messenger and protector. They have the best eyesight of all the birds of prey and hold the energy of visionaries of the air. They can awaken your visionary power and help you find your life purpose.

How to Connect With "Outside of Me"

How do you use your intuition with your angels, spirit guides, DLOs (Deceased Loved Ones) and so on? All of these beings are always there to help you only if you ask for their help. These guides generally will not communicate or interfere with your life unless you ask them to. The only exception may be your passed loved ones or DLOs. Often our DLOs will send us signs and signals that they are still around even after they have passed to tell you that they are okay and love you. My grandfather, after he died at age 101 would turn the dial on the radio in the bathroom back to his favorite channel even though my aunt, whom he lived with, had changed it to a different one. Every time she changed it to a station she wanted to listen to, it would mysteriously change back to Grandpa's favorite. He was just telling her he's still around.

The first step to use your intuition to connect to "outside of me" is to believe your guides and angels are really there and then to ask them to help you. They cannot assist you without your asking for their help since they cannot interfere with your free will. The only exception is when your well-being or life is in mortal danger. Being messengers of God and providing you divine guidance, they will then give you answers to your questions with gentle guidance through your intuition. You can enhance your awareness and connection with your angels through some simple practice.

The simple steps to receiving guidance messages are to ask, receive and give thanks. This is very similar to the Intuition On Demand Technique, the difference is your intention to receive divine guidance from your guides. You ask for help in the form of a question, a prayer or a desire.

Here are the steps:

1. Simply ask. Ask in your mind or aloud for the assistance or guidance you need. Do not be afraid to ask for anything, even something simple. If you do not know what to ask, you can ask for guidance on what to do next for your highest good.

2. Receive. Receiving is the allowing of the messages to come to you in whatever form they may appear. This is the same as Be Open. Do not try to anticipate how you will receive an answer, but know that it will come and be on the lookout for it. Through your intuition the response will be immediate.

3. Give Thanks. After you received an answer or a message, give thanks and appreciation for the divine guidance you've been given. You can give thanks to your angels, to God, The Universe or just give thanks in general.

You may continue to receive guidance over the next few days or weeks. Be on the lookout for a sign! Often guidance can be readily seen through synchronicities, those funny incidents in life that seem to be relevant answers to our questions. You may see a sign or a license plate with a name or a word that has meaning to you. You may be listening to the radio, or surfing on the web, and a video or a song pops up that has lyrics with the answer you need. Perhaps an advertisement has words that seem to have relevance to your question or need. These are external signs and messages are given to us from our guides.

Remember, you just need to ask for help, or ask a question in your mind, which is good enough. You can speak out loud your question or request, or you can write them a letter. I have always liked Automatic Angel Writing for communicating with my angels. Building your relationship with them is key! It is not that they need to get to know you, but you need to get to know them and when you receive messages constantly and consistently your trust in them will grow. They already know you. You've just forgotten them. Everything you are learning here is about how to connect with divine guidance using your intuition. You merely have to have the intent to receive divine guidance from divine sources when you use your intuition.

Highlighted Tips and Summary

- Believing in something outside of yourself that is the source of your intuitive messages can help you access your intuition more easily.
- You don't have to be religious to connect to assistance outside of you.
- If you want to receive guidance from sources outside of you, such as angels and spirit guides, you can follow these three steps:

Simply Ask — Receive — Give Thanks

These steps overlay the Intuition On Demand Technique, so you can include them when connecting to your intuition.

CHAPTER 16

Meditation and Intuition

• • • • • • • • • • • • •

In intuition development, one of the most frequently mentioned things to strengthen your intuition is meditation. Every teacher and book on intuition development I've encountered talks about the importance of meditation for developing an ability to detect and receive your intuitive messages. Meditation is an elusive but highly prized activity held in high regard as being the best thing for intuition. At the same time, the word meditation often makes people cringe and want to run away.

Many people struggle with meditation because most people don't know how to truly meditate or say they've tried to meditate but can't. The main complaint is they can't still their mind during meditation, or they find it boring and a chore because they have to repeat a mantra or a word. The truth is you don't need to still your mind or repeat a mantra to meditate. Even better, you don't have to meditate for a long time to get immediate and long lasting effects to boost your intuition.

With nearly 40 years experience in meditation and having studied the brain science of meditation, I discovered surprising facts about what meditation truly is.

What Real Meditation Is

First, meditation is not a religious practice though it is often used as part of a daily spiritual exercise. Meditation, in one form or another is found in many beliefs and practices. Meditation is defined as a mental exercise designed to promote relaxation and enhance physical and emotional well-being. From a spiritual standpoint, many religions believe that meditation can lead us to God, and the Hindus say, "Only in meditation can we see the inner Self directly."

When I teach meditation in a class, the first thing people say to me is, "I tried to meditate, but I can't." I discovered they had a common problem that I also had when I first started meditating. The problem is a misconception over just how to meditate and what your state of mind is supposed to be in during meditation. When I began meditating many years ago, I went through a lot of frustration and confusion with my own meditation. I wasn't quite sure what I was supposed to do, or not do. I had heard comments like, "Make your mind a blank," or, "You have to focus your mind." I wasn't quite sure what either of those meant. I wanted to meditate because I knew there were amazing benefits to meditating, one of which was better intuitive skills and the other was enlightenment. Now, who wouldn't want enlightenment? After learning several meditation methods and then studying the brain science behind meditation, it became clearer as to what the meditation experience should feel like and how to get into it.

You actually go into a meditative state every time you fall asleep, even though it is brief. It is that twilight feeling where you are just about to go into slumber but you are still a bit aware of your surroundings though it may seem farther away. You also are in this state just before you wake up fully from sleeping. A meditation technique puts your mind in this state of awareness through relaxing you and then keeps you there without falling asleep.

You can also be in a meditative state when you are doing a simple task that requires some attention but is somewhat repetitive, like driving, walking, doing the dishes, or folding your laundry. This puts you in a state of focused attention. When you are in a state of focused attention this, to some extent, stills your mind.

Meditation is a relaxed mind and body where you have the attention of the "witness." This means that you are noticing or witnessing what is going on in your mind but you are not attaching yourself to the thoughts that go by. You're not allowing these free-floating thoughts to grab your mind and trigger your thinking about them. For example, you begin to meditate and then your mind thinks, "Oh, I need to send out that email to my friend," or "I forgot to put eggs on my shopping list." When this happens, you let those thoughts go by and don't get up from meditation, but let go of letting those thoughts cascade you into a series of more thoughts such as, "...and while I'm writing that email, I need to include such and such and so and so," or "oh and I also need milk on my shopping list to make that cake I wanted to bake." Just stop and go back to your meditation technique. Meditation is not stopping your mind from having these free-floating thoughts, but allowing them to come and go without hanging on to them.

The key to quieting your mind is focusing your attention on something that is simple and repetitive. At the same time the process should relax both your mind and your body without falling into a deep sleep. You may feel like you're drifting off to sleep, but you aren't quite asleep, you are still aware. It may also seem like you're dreaming, but you are still awake. You'll be very relaxed and you're aware of the room you're in but it feels like the room is more in the distance. You may see images or have thoughts that pop up that you don't have control over and you're not thinking them through.

It is perfectly fine for these images to come up. In fact, this is where you may find your epiphanies or your intuitive insights! You will feel like you may be dreaming these images but you know you are not, you are still consciously aware. For example, you may still hear people talking around you but do not know exactly what is being said. Again, it almost feels like a distant awareness. You may feel your body having sensations of lightness, numbness or floating. You may feel bliss. All these feelings are okay and are similar to what you feel when you are about to fall asleep.

This process of relaxing and focusing our attention brings us into a meditative state and the more you practice, the deeper you can go into meditation which allows you to access the Theta and Delta brain wave states of consciousness.

What Does Real Meditation Feel Like?

Anna Wise, the author of *The High-Performance Mind,* is an authority on measuring brain waves during meditation. By looking at the brain waves of meditators that are associated with different states of consciousness, she gives us some idea of what it feels like when you're meditating. The four major brain states are:

- **Beta** – The state of being awake, thinking and consciously aware.
- **Alpha** – A relaxed detached awareness, usually when you are daydreaming.
- **Theta** – You are fully asleep and dreaming, your subconscious is active and you can easily receive intuitive messages.
- **Delta** - You are unconscious or in deep sleep and it is believed this state is connected to Universal Consciousness.

When you fall asleep you go through all four states of consciousness from Beta to Alpha, then Theta and Delta. Wise's research has shown that as we meditate, our minds go through the same states of consciousness. The only difference is that in meditation, you remain aware of what is going on in your mind as you pass through those different states and you don't reach the Delta state. We can have all four brain waves present when we are awake as well. All of these brain waves are mixed in different proportions. When you are awake you have more Beta waves, and almost no Delta waves; when you are in deep sleep you have lots of Delta and no Beta. You want to meditate such that you have more Theta and less Beta brain waves but still be awake.

Meditation trains our mind to stay aware while going through other states of consciousness that are associated with these different brain waves. To remain awake you need some Beta awareness as you go through Alpha, Theta and even into the Delta states of mind. This all happens naturally when you fall asleep and meditate, so you don't need to try to be awake while you're in meditation, it won't work. If you do try to stay awake you'll just remain in the Beta state of consciousness.

Why and How Meditation Works for Intuition

When you begin to witness things going through your mind, whether it is your free-floating thoughts, random images, or just sounds drifting through your mind, you will become more aware of your intuitive pop-ups. Meditation techniques automatically reduce your thinking by giving you something to focus on that is repetitive and purposely not thought stimulating. The more your mind quiets, coupled with physical relaxation, the more you become present and aware of being in "the now." Being in "the now" is being more aware of what is around you and also how you are feeling at the moment. If you are thinking of the future or the past, you are not in "the now." By being more in "the now" you become more aware of what pops up in your mind.

This will help you become aware of your intuition and your intuitive mind as it pops up messages in the same way. Remember, your intuitive mind is more in "the now" and is very subtle. So you need to quiet your thinking mind to hear your intuition's subtle pop-up messages. This is how meditation helps develop your intuition. Working with meditation helped me go from not being able to "see" images in my mind to becoming highly clairvoyant, receiving intuitive messages through images almost all the time. It wasn't only because I meditated, but also because of what I learned by practicing how to meditate. Here's how it happened.

I learned how to meditate when I was fourteen years old. I learned a mantra meditation where you repeat a mantra, which is just a word, over and over again. It wasn't too hard and I could certainly just sit with my eyes closed and repeat a word. Now, being a dutiful student I was really good at this, repeating the word over and over slowly. Every time my mind would wander, and I noticed it, I'd bring it back to repeat my mantra word. I pushed everything out of my mind to stick to the mantra. I was quite good at it and practiced meditating every day for 15-20 minutes in the morning.

Then in college a group of students in my psychology class got together to meditate in the new small, but empty planetarium, in the science building. It was a nice round room with a carpeted floor and soft offset lighting, which was just perfect for meditating. Most of us sat on the floor, some lay down, and others brought meditation cushions to sit on. I sat as I usually did and settled in to get ready to meditate, repeating my mantra for the 20 minutes as we all meditated together. When the lights came slowly up and everyone stirred coming out of their meditations we began to share our meditation experiences. Some were saying how blissful it was. Quite a few were having visions and seeing colors. A couple of them spoke about how they were transported on a journey and saw all kinds of wonderful heavenly places. When I meditated, all I saw was black. I was surprised and disappointed that others were having great visual experiences and I saw nothing. I thought I was really good at meditating! Was I doing something wrong?

It turns out that I was actually bringing myself out of meditation by being such a good girl, being awake and alert, to make sure I was sticking to the mantra. If I started to drift into that twilight state and stop repeating the mantra, I would "wake" up and start repeating my mantra again. Each time I did this I would pull myself out of true meditation. Once I understood what I was doing, I was not so quick to destroy what was coming up in my mind during meditation, but allow it to be noticed and then go by. I didn't hang on to those things. I then realized I had been pushing out of my mind the images that were popping up in my mind the instant I thought they were intruding on my mantra.

The images weren't always complete and sometimes a bit odd. One was a dog that was made up of tiny little iridescent balls of multicolored light that pulsated and scintillated. The images flashed and then went away. It surprised me and that's why I remember it. Another time I saw a double hung multi-pane window with bright green leaves from a tree on a bright sunny day showing through it. The images were a little startling making me think, "Whoa! What was that?" I wasn't used to these random odd images.

This made me realize that I do have images in my mind, I just never noticed them. I continued to meditate and allow those images to come up, notice them and let them go. This was the beginning of seeing intuitive images as they too popped up in the same way when I was not meditating. I was also able to now recognize images in my mind, whereas before I didn't notice that I had images in my mind. Being able to notice those images when I was not meditating is what helped me become very clairvoyant.

The purpose of the mantra is to keep your mind centered on one thing as you relax and allow your mind to go through the different states of consciousness. It also allows you to remain aware like a witness that just observes as you enter into the Theta state. Eventually, the mantra fades away as you enter this state but you are still aware and not sleeping. It's a very peaceful, calm and blissful feeling. If you can get your mind there, you may like it so much you want to keep it there longer. Once you are able to get into this state of meditation your mind is now aware of the intuition pop-ups that float through your mind all the time. Your thinking mind has quieted down and you are in a state of relaxed awareness. Meditation gives you the experience and the practice of being aware of your intuitive mind.

Meditation Benefits

Many of the benefits of meditation have now been proven in both science and medicine. Scientific research done at Harvard, Yale and MIT discovered that meditation increases the gray matter of the brain, which is the part of the brain you use for higher thinking. They found the increase was greater in older people than young, which suggests that meditation may slow down the deterioration of the brain as we age and improve brain function. Other studies have shown that even if you meditate only for ten minutes a day you can gain positive benefits by changing the wiring in your brain for the better permanently!

Meditation has been shown to:

- Reduce anxiety, depression and stress.
- Reduce heart disease.
- Help weight loss.
- Help reduce addictions.
- Help reduce asthma.
- Improve immunity.
- Improve focus and concentration.
- Build self-confidence.
- Enhance physical energy and strength.
- Develop your intuitive abilities.
- The best of all, meditation can lead to *ENLIGHTENMENT*.

How to Meditate to Improve Your Intuition

Now that you have a better understanding of what meditation is, here is how you can meditate to improve your intuition as well as gain many other benefits. Just by getting yourself to sit even for a few moments and turn your attention to your body and how you are feeling is a great start to quieting your mind. By merely closing your eyes your attention is already drawn inward and makes it easier for you to focus your attention on relaxing and being present. Keep in mind that meditation is all about what you are paying attention to. You don't need to sit in a lotus position or in any special cross-legged position. You don't need to sit on the floor either. You can meditate in bed, though it's better to start sitting. You can meditate anywhere, any time, except when you need to be alert and interact in some activity, like driving. Don't meditate when you're driving.

First you'll want to choose a kind of meditation to follow. There are different kinds of meditations that range from what I would call beginner to advanced. It doesn't matter what kind of meditation you do as long as you can get into that meditative state which is similar to when you are just about to fall asleep but you're still aware. All of these meditation methods are meant to bring your attention back to a "thing," which can be a story being told to you, a mantra or your breathing. This quiets your thinking mind and helps you fall into a relaxed state of awareness, which is meditating.

The easiest meditations are called guided meditations. This is where you follow spoken instructions to help you relax and then guides you through imagining a story or takes you on a journey. The guidance gives you something to pay attention to and if your mind wanders you remind yourself to come back to listening to the meditation guide. If you don't know where to get a guided meditation you can go to my website for some meditations in the product section or you can search for them on the web.

The next level of meditation is a mantra meditation. A mantra is just a sound, word or phrase that is repeated over and over again. The mantra is not said aloud but rather repeated in your mind. In Eastern philosophies a mantra is often the name of God or phrases that are considered sacred. In a mantra meditation it is often easiest to synchronize the mantra with your breathing. So when you inhale you repeat your mantra, and when you exhale you say your mantra. Remember the mantra is repeated in your mind, not verbally. If your mind wanders from the mantra, just gently bring it back to focus on repeating your mantra. You can pick any word or phrase you'd like to repeat. It can be "Om" or it can be an affirmation such as, "I am love." You can use any word you'd like even a simple word like, "pencil." I was taught the phrase "Om Namah Shivaya" meaning in sanskrit "I bow to the God within me as me," to use as a mantra.

An intermediate level meditation is to follow your breath by paying attention to your breathing. You follow your breath in as you inhale and follow it out as you exhale. This becomes a bit harder to pay attention to since it is very simple, so if your mind wanders, you may need to remind yourself to come back to your breath more often. There's often a larger pause between exhaling then inhaling as opposed to inhaling then exhaling, which is fine. The key here is to pay attention to your breaths as they go in and out. If your mind wanders you just gently bring it back to focusing on your breathing. The great thing about this meditation is that you are always breathing so it keeps going even if you get distracted and will be there for you to come back to.

The most advanced meditation method is to focus on the silent pauses between your breaths. By focusing on the silence between your breaths you are putting your attention on being the witness and not the participant. You can start by becoming aware of your breathing as you inhale the coolness of the air coming in, and then the warmth of the air that passes through your nose as you exhale. If your thoughts start to intrude, just let them go by, do not follow them. You may be tempted to abandon your breath and think about the thoughts or feelings arising but let them go. As you pay attention to your inhale and then exhale, notice the pause between them. There is a slight pause of silence at the moment just before you inhale or exhale. Focus on each pause of silence.

⁓

So let's get ready to meditate now that you know the different types of meditation methods there are. Choose one that you're comfortable with. When you are ready to meditate try to find a place that is quiet where you won't be disturbed. You may want to turn off your phone ringer and notifications so you can't be distracted. You'll want to be able to sit comfortably with your back straight and your feet flat on the floor. You can put your hands in your lap in a way that is comfortable for you. I usually place my right hand in my left, which happens to be a position that Buddha would place his hands in during meditation. You can use cushions if it helps support your sitting up.

Here is a simple relaxation-breathing meditation you can do for intuition. Read it through first then try it for a few minutes or as long as you can.

1. Gently close your eyes.
2. Relax and take several long, slow, deep breaths.
3. Breathe normally and pay attention to yourself inhaling and then exhaling for a few breaths.
4. Turn your attention to your body; notice the tension you may feel in your head, neck, body, arms or legs.
5. Start with the top of your head and allow your awareness to move down your body; as you notice an area of tension, with every breath, relax that area of tense muscle one at a time.
6. As you feel more relaxed, just follow your breathing, as you breathe in and out.
7. If your mind wanders to thinking, gently bring your awareness back to your inhale and exhale.
8. As you pay attention to your breathing, notice the air as it moves gently in and out through your nose. Don't try to breathe, just follow your natural breathing pattern, which will slow down normally.

9. Follow your breathing until you feel you are ready or want to come out of meditation.
10. When you are ready to come out of meditation, come back to being aware of yourself sitting in the room and slowly, when you're ready, open your eyes.

If you find this hard to do for a few minutes, then just try it for 30 seconds. After a while you may be surprised how deeply you are meditating, so take your time "coming back" to your fully awake self before you open your eyes.

To start you may just want to try any meditation for a few minutes in the beginning to get used to sitting still and feeling what it is like to meditate. A short meditation of 2-3 minutes is fine, then you can work your way up to ten and even twenty minutes, which is ideal. If you can and want to meditate longer, say for an hour that is fine. Meditate once a day for the best results. It does not matter what time of day you meditate as long as you are able to find a quiet place where you won't be disturbed or tempted to get up and do something else.

As you meditate longer you may feel a little numb just as you do when you start to wake up from sleeping. You may hear people speaking but you don't know what they're saying and that is okay. You may lose track of the guided meditation narration and no longer hear the words but you know you are not sleeping. This is fine as well. Keep in mind that the meditative state feels like you are just about to fall asleep, but you don't. You are still aware and conscious but also calm and relaxed. You may feel a little buzzy when you come out of meditation and this is okay too. Just give yourself time to come back to being fully awake and conscious.

You will probably find that meditation feels great and gives you a much better rest than if you went to bed for a cat nap. Meditating into your afternoon nap will put you in a deeper state of rest and rejuvenation than just snoozing.

FAQ about Meditation

1. Can I meditate lying down? Yes, you can as long as you don't fall asleep.
2. Do I have to have a special room for meditation? No, you don't but having the same place, chair or room for meditation is very

helpful to get into the meditative state more quickly as you meditate more and more.

3. Do I have to sit in a special posture to have a better meditation? No, as mentioned before you don't need to sit in a special position, such as a lotus cross-legged posture.

4. How do I choose a good guided meditation? It is important that you pick a voice in the guided meditation that you like to listen to. You may not want music that is complicated or not relaxing. The voice and music should have sounds that are soothing to you and don't change much in terms of loudness or rhythm.

5. Suppose I fall asleep? If you fall asleep that's okay, it probably means you are really tired. That being said, you should then get more rest so when you do meditate you don't fall asleep!

6. When I meditate I feel incredibly anxious or mentally uncomfortable, what should I do? I would suggest you stop meditating if it is too mentally uncomfortable for you to do.

PART FIVE

Your Intuitive Life

CHAPTER 17

How to Take Your Intuition Home with You and FAQ

• • • • • • • • • • • • •

A question I often hear my students ask is, "How do I stay tuned into my intuition and receive messages from my inner divine guidance?" They do very well in class and in the online sessions but when they go off on their own, life takes over and they feel disconnected. The answer to how to "be intuitive" all the time is to learn how to lead an intuitive life. Part of this is learning to create a habit of remembering to use your intuition. Another part is to learn to live a more intuitive life!

Being Intuitive - The Intuitive Life

What does it mean to be intuitive? It means to work with your intuition all the time, but that's easy because your intuition is always on and sending you information. It is also reminding yourself that you can employ your intuition to help you for anything, and then actually using it! To be intuitive you have to live more of an intuitive life and here are a few ways how to do that.

Pay Attention To Your Intuition

Now you are well educated in how your intuition sends you messages. As you practice using your intuition and doing proper intuition exercises, you will begin to discover more about how your intuition presents you information through hearing, seeing, feeling and thoughts either inside or outside of you. When you're talking to someone, as you pause to listen to their response be open and pay attention to not only their words but also to what pop-ups arise in you. If you are out and about, as you are walking or standing somewhere pay attention to what you are feeling. Remember that your intuition is always sending you signals and information. You can pay more attention to your intuition if you allow yourself to "Be Open" just as you would be in the second step of the Intuition On Demand Technique. By giving yourself some time to stop and be open at various times in your day, you'll create a habit of noticing your intuition more, even when you are not trying to notice it. Your intuition will be noticeable automatically. Cultivate that awareness by reminding yourself that your intuition is sending you signals at any time. You just need to remind yourself that a feeling that suddenly arises may be one of those signals. Perhaps a sudden thought pops up that has the characteristics of an intuitive thought; it's short, to the point, neutral and makes a statement.

In my earlier story about the "green car" I had heard just the words, "Get behind the green car." I wasn't quite sure where it was coming from, I didn't have much time to analyze if it was my intuition popping up or not, but I followed it anyway because it was repetitive and to the point. There was no harm in following it and realized later it was my intuition and could have caused me a lot of harm if I hadn't followed it. You may get pop-up intuitive thoughts that tell you to go this way instead of that, or to pick up that book and read it. No harm in following it and all the benefits may await you.

The more you practice your intuition exercises, the clearer it will be for you on how your intuition does come to you in both sight, sound, thoughts and feelings. If you are diligent in journaling your intuition exercise hits and your stories of when you received hits with your intuition, you'll reinforce in your mind what it is like when your intuition is communicating with you. Then it becomes easier for you to notice your intuition and in this way make intuitive messages stand out for you.

Deliberately Use Your Intuition in Decision-Making

Actually setting your intention to use your intuition whenever you can and on whatever you do is the best way to keep actively engaged with your intuition. I had to train myself to remember to use my intuition with my normal decision-making process to help me decide. Usually, I remembered to use my intuition only when I was stuck trying to choose between two things that were fairly equal. Many times it wasn't a big decision. Once I remembered to use my intuition and the results were good it helped me build a habit to use my intuition on all my decisions, and it has become second nature. Using your intuition to help make a decision doesn't mean that you throw out using your logic and thinking mind to decide. You can combine your logic with your intuition in decision-making.

You are always making decisions and there are always new things or changes coming into your life. These are all opportunities to use your intuition. When the mail comes, whether it's physical mail or email, you can use your intuition to predict what kind of mail will come, how many bills, or how many emails from friends or spam? When you walk into a public bathroom use your intuition to choose the best stall to use. You enter a waiting room and have to choose a place to sit; use your intuition to pick!

Find opportunities to use your intuition. One day I was going to a restaurant for dinner with my husband. I had made an early reservation on the computer. When we entered the restaurant the tables were mostly empty. The hostess said, "You can pick any place you want to sit." Ah! This was an opportunity to use my intuition. You can do this too, if you have to pick a place to sit in a restaurant; scan the room and at the same time ask, "Where is the best place for me to sit?" See where you are drawn to, which table or chair feels right to you. Perhaps one area seems brighter to you and more inviting, or more cozy. Some areas may make you feel repulsed; so don't go in that direction. In this case, I was drawn to a particular table in the corner and picked that one. The hostess said, "Funny, that's the table that the computer had picked for you." What a pleasant surprise, I gather my intuition was right! You can further validate whether your intuitive choice was correct by seeing how you feel once you sit at your table. Is it comfortable? You may find that later some rather unpleasant people or things happen near the table that you felt repulsed by. That is validation too. These are all great examples of opportunities to practice using your intuition as well as use it purposefully.

Develop Your Intuition By Going Further

You've just started to develop your intuition by reading this book. You can go much further as we have just scratched the surface. This is merely the beginning of how far you can go with getting detailed and extensive intuitive information. As with any other skill, to really be good at it you have to keep working at it and learning more. There are a few things you can do to go further with your intuition.

Becoming more sensitive to your body and your heart you can strengthen your ability to connect to your intuition more easily. Your heart is the strongest electromagnetic field generator in the body. Your heart allows your intentions, via thought and emotional energy, to reach farther and be able to connect more strongly to the energy around you.

By being compassionate, by having sympathy and empathy for others you are connecting to your heart. It's been found that when you connect with your heart to someone or something you can more easily pick up intuitive information about them.

You can participate in activities that require you to use your intuition. It may be a creative activity such as art, photography, interior decorating, fashion or even putting together your own website. Then remember to use your intuition when doing these activities. When I create my newsletters I use my intuition to select the photos I'm going to use even though I'm not an artist. I will still try to connect to my intuitive side.

Another way you can go further with developing your intuition is to get together with like-minds. Finding other people who have similar interests to yours and are also looking to develop their intuition. Just finding people who even believe in the power of intuition is a big step towards lifting up your attitude about being intuitive and feel good about working on improving yours. Since the value in using your intuition deliberately is still seen by some as unusual, weird or silly, it may make you feel ashamed or want to hide that you are developing your intuition. This is why it is important to find like-minds to be with. You want to surround yourself with people who will support you and encourage you to keep going. Find a class or a group to join that is developing their intuition or is filled with intuitive people. Taking a class on intuition development helps you connect to others who are in the same boat as you and may want to practice with you.

Working with energy can be a great way to build on your intuition skills. Learning how to do energy healing can be helpful since many modalities rely on intuition as part of their protocol. In fact, many QiGong protocols for healing often use intuition.

Even if you don't want to be an intuitive reader for the public, doing intuitive readings for your friends or family, if they are open to it, can be helpful to improve your intuition. While you may know a lot about your friends and family, you don't know everything and can still do intuitive readings for them. You can do these readings for fun and that will also help you work to improve your intuition by taking off some performance pressure.

Practice Makes Clarity

It is truly worth mentioning again how important intuition practice is so you can grow your intuition skills. Just doing the exercises once through and then trying to use your intuition on important life decisions will result in disappointment. You won't be able to receive clear intuitive messages because you haven't honed your skill. Keep in mind that like learning any new skill it requires work! I have seen students go through a basic course, or just learn the intuition technique, and then try to use their intuition on life decisions they are trying to make. This is similar to learning how to ski, and having just gotten beginner instructions then trying to go down the advanced trail on the mountain!

Practice, practice, practice makes clarity. Many times people complain that they can't tell the difference between their intuition and whether they are making it up, or they are not even sure whether their intuition is telling them something. When you experience your intuition many times, over and over again, you notice how it comes to you in all its flavors and characteristics. This is how it usually develops for everyone.

My students go through similar experiences. One student said she gets her intuitive hits and information even before she gets a chance to ask her intuition a question. When she started doing her first intuition exercises she realized she would see flashes of images immediately before she took the first step in the technique. She just merely needed to set her intention to do the exercise and her intuition would give her information. By practicing many intuition exercises she found a consistency in how those images popped up instantly the moment she was ready to do the exercise, so she began to expect them. As she shared more of her intuitive image flashes she also realized that she had some feelings that went along with them. These particular intuitive images were great hits. By exercising her intuition and remembering how her intuitive hits come to her, she was able to recognize them when they came in and pick up more detail and information. This is how the intuitive experience develops. This is also how you can get more detailed information from your intuition.

It is important to practice as often as you can. I make no apology for having repeated this throughout this book; you have to practice. You can practice on your own and as mentioned there are infinite opportunities to practice using your intuition in simple ways in life. You can practice with your friends who are willing to partner with you. You can also join a development circle in person or online. It's important that you keep practicing and it is best to practice with other people, if possible.

Staying Tuned In

You may want to stay connected to a higher power, your higher self, your angels, All That Is and/or divine guidance. How do you stay tuned in and connected all the time? It starts with your state of mind, then working with your energy, journaling and meditation.

States of Mind

Your state of mind is key to staying connected and tuning into your intuition all the time. If you can work with your mind to be able to come back and center yourself, you'll be able to be calm in both your mind and body.

You can do this by spending time in sacred spaces. This can be a special place that you set up for yourself in your home where you meditate or pray. Just by spending time in this special place helps remind you to turn within and focus on your own spirituality. If you belong to a church, temple or other place of worship, that certainly can be your place to go to contemplate and come to center yourself. Places of worship or your own spiritual place purposely exist to remind us of our spirituality and reconnect. A sacred space can also be a special place in nature, or natural location that brings you a sense of grandeur and spirit. When you are in a sacred space relax and absorb the energy and feeling there. You will bring it with you wherever you go.

Positive intentions, affirmations, prayer help put your mind in a less worried, less stressed mind. It may also calm a busy mind. Prayers are positive intentions that are hope in words. When you pray your angels come immediately to your awareness if you are open and set the Universe's energy in motion to answer them.

Energy Health

Remember to keep both your physical and metaphysical energy up, positive, and healthy. We have gone over how to do this earlier in the book. Go exercise, walk, breathe in fresh air, get your blood oxygenated by getting it flowing. Eat well and reduce your intake of processed foods. This is all good for your body and health as well, which will help your intuition and staying connected.

Journaling

It's important that you journal your intuition experiences. Journaling can be great to keep track of your intuition hits so you can remember how it comes to you. In addition, journaling in a diary your free thoughts it can be helpful to talk to your inner guidance as someone that is not you.

Meditation

The last piece to staying connected is to meditate. Meditate as often as you can even if it is for a few minutes a day. The best way to be consistent with meditation is to find a time that fits into your daily schedule that is convenient for you. Then meditate at that time every day. Habits take 30 days to become part of your automatic routine.

Frequently Asked Questions

In my travels speaking and teaching I've come across many people who ask the same common questions. You may have the same questions, so they are listed here.

Q When is it my intuition and when am I making it up?
A If you have an emotional attachment to the message you are receiving then you are coming from your Ego and Left Brain, which is not intuitive. Your true intuitive messages should come to you in a calm and unemotional way. Even in situations where a message is helping you in a crisis or warning you of danger, it will be calm, supportive and unemotional. If the message is vague and confusing then it is not a true message. True messages are clear, short and to the point.

Q I'm not getting much when I try to use my intuition. I just receive a few things and not much else; is my intuition working?
A Your intuition is working because it is always working. You're always thinking, feeling, seeing, hearing and this is how your intuition communicates to you. If you feel that you aren't getting much it can be caused by two things. First, trying too hard or having performance anxiety often causes this. So let it go, you can stop trying to get a message. A teacher can give you techniques to reduce your performance anxiety. The second is that you are anticipating your intuitive message to come to you in a particular way, and you missed how it actually did present itself.

Q Sometimes the things I get are wrong. What should I do?

A That's okay. As you develop you will get things that are seemingly not right. The best thing to do is to let it go and don't hang onto it. You get what you get and you don't get upset. Press on and practice.

Q How do I know what … so and so … means?

A If you don't know what your intuition is giving you, you can ask another question to trigger your intuition to give you more information. If it still doesn't make sense then let it go.

Q Sometimes I see animals show up everywhere, what does that mean?

A It may be your animal guide, or a symbol. You can ask your intuition why you are being shown that particular animal and what the meaning of it is.

Q When I try to use my intuition I don't getting anything, my mind is a blank.

A You are always getting something, again, because you are always seeing, feeling, hearing, and thinking. You may be looking for your intuition to come to you in a particular way and you miss how it is actually giving you messages. What can help is to work with a teacher who can help show you how to analyze what you have received to determine what is a message and what isn't.

Q What do I do if I receive messages for other people or strangers?

A The best thing is to keep that message to yourself, particularly when you are just starting out to learn how to develop your intuition and psychic skills. As you become more advanced you'll know what the best thing is to do, because you can ask your intuition and know when you're getting a clear answer. But, it is generally better not to intrude on others, particularly if they are strangers. The Universe will get a message to them if needed, and you are not necessarily the messenger.

Q What if I get something that is upsetting or scary?

A Then it probably is not a true intuitive message because intuition comes subtly and won't scare you.

Q Should I be afraid of negative energies?

A Not if you set an intention to only bring in divine energy and messages from your guides and angels that naturally protect you. Also, working with the metaphysical energy techniques taught earlier, to clear and raise your energy, will help here.

Q Do you feel that going organic as well as eating just all natural foods will increase your intuition?

A I don't believe that you must be vegetarian to be more intuitive. I do think in general, being in a healthier way, whichever is healthier for you, does help you in every aspect of your being, mentally and physically. I believe that if God meant for humans to be vegetarians we wouldn't be able to eat meat. We are omnivores, not herbivores.

Q How can a person tell, or what might we anticipate, when our intuition rings true? What types of "signs or symptoms" might a person experience?

A There are definite signs and symptoms of true intuition. Your intuition speaks to you in a few words, an urge or feeling that is not scary, non-threatening and often quietly repetitive. Then you can use an intuition technique to check your intuition's message, which you can also practice, which makes it easier and faster to recognize your intuition when she speaks to you.

Q I sometimes struggle with telling fear from intuition. Fear seems to cloud things at times.

A Fear does cloud intuition. To deal with your fear I found using intuition tools help get you out of that space of fear so you can receive intuitive messages more clearly.

Q Is intuition a true physical feeling inside, which I sometimes have? Or that little voice in your head?

A Intuition can be both the physical feeling inside and the little voice in your head, which is not your Ego or thinking mind.

Final Thoughts

There are infinite possibilities of wonderful and exciting things you can bring into your life being highly intuitive. From creating a happier and more fulfilled life to possibly even spiritual enlightenment awaits you when you develop your intuition skills. Remember, everyone can be highly intuitive. There is no exception to this because it is part of your biology and is a gift given to everyone. I have confidence in you that you can improve your intuition greatly with persistence, practice and the techniques you've learned in this book.

Don't give up. It does take time, but the more you use it the faster it will improve and bring you results.

Helping you become intuitive so you can live a better life with the assistance of intuitive guidance is why I do this. If we all were living lives guided by our inner voice trusting that it is giving us divine guidance, how wonderful our lives and the world would be.

All through history humans have sought a better way to live through connecting to a greater source of knowledge that is beyond them. In the ever-changing events of our world today we all feel a great need to find solace, comfort and steady guidance to carry us through life. It is my deep desire to help everyone live a better life through his or her own amazing intuitive guidance. I hope this practical guide will help you to develop your intuition and so enrich and enhance your life and those of others.

Acknowledgements

I want to thank all of my fans, followers, students and friends who inspired me to create this book. You were the ones who encouraged me to write a book on intuition. I dedicate this book to all of you.

Thank you to Sabine, Thierry, Gail my publicist and Michael my editor at Findhorn Press for supporting this book and helping get it out to the world. Your kindness is overwhelming. My deepest gratitude goes to my parents who always taught me to be open, look beyond, and the importance of spirituality in life. All of which set me on a quest to learn as much as I can about the world. Particularly to my Dad who taught me how the world works through science and his stories of his own mystical experiences that started my fascination with both. Thank you Mom and Dad for your unconditional love and your undying belief in me.

Thank you to my now adult son, Christopher, who has become my go to person for grammar, punctuation and anything to do with language. Finally, thank you to my wonderful husband, Vincent, who is the love of my life. I am forever grateful for your love and unending support in all that I do.